KARMA and REINCARNATION

KARMA and REINCARNATION

Transcending Your Past,
Transforming Your Future

ELIZABETH CLARE PROPHET
and **PATRICIA R. SPADARO**

SUMMIT UNIVERSITY ✸ PRESS®

KARMA AND REINCARNATION
Transcending Your Past, Transforming Your Future
by Elizabeth Clare Prophet and Patricia R. Spadaro
Copyright © 2001 Summit Publications, Inc.
All rights reserved. Second edition 2004

Library of Congress Catalog Number: 00-110853
ISBN: 0-922729-61-1

SUMMIT UNIVERSITY ♥ PRESS

Printed in the United States of America.
09   08   07   06   05   6   5   4   3   2

Contents

Note: Because gender-neutral language can be cumbersome and at times confusing, we have often used *he* and *him* to refer to God or the individual. These terms are for readability only and are not intended to exclude women or the feminine aspect of the Godhead. Likewise, our use of *God* or *Spirit* does not exclude other expressions for the Divine.

Karmic Conundrums

Luck is a word devoid of sense.
Nothing can exist without a cause.
                              —VOLTAIRE

The word *karma* has made it into the mainstream. Just look at bumper stickers like *My karma ran over your dogma* or *It's a thankless job, but I've got a lot of karma to burn off*. But not everyone understands what karma really means, why it matters and how to deal with it.

Think about the talents you were born with and the good things that have happened to you in life. Now think about the so-called limitations and challenges that have come your way. Both have to do with your karma. Karma simply tells us that what happens to us in the present is the result of causes we ourselves have set in motion in the past—whether ten minutes ago or ten lifetimes ago.

We've all grown up learning about karma. We just didn't call it that. Instead we heard: *What goes around comes around. Whatsoever a man soweth, that shall he also reap. For every action there is an equal and opposite reaction. And in the end, the love you take is equal to the love you make.* In essence, karma tells us that whatever we do will come full circle to our doorstep—sometime, somewhere.

Karma and reincarnation go hand in hand. While karma means accountability and payback, reincarnation is simply another word for opportunity. Reincarnation gives us another chance to make good on the karmic debts we owe others and to reap the blessings we have sent forth.

Karma and reincarnation also help us make sense out of the question marks in life. *Why me? Why not me?* Why was my niece born with Down's syndrome when her brothers and sisters are healthy and robust? Why have I been blessed with promotion after promotion while my brother can't hold down a job—even though we had the same opportunities growing up? Why do all my relationships become a tug of war—how come I can't live with him and I can't live without him? Why, when I just landed the job I've been after for a year, do I have to leave town to care for my ailing parents? Why did I survive a car accident when all of my friends in the car were killed?

Life is full of paradoxes and questions like these. Like a Zen koan, each paradox is designed to make us dig deeper, connect with our inner soul knowing and solve the karmic conundrum.

Taking a Cue from Nature

Come forth into the light of things,
Let Nature be your teacher.
　　　　　　　—WILLIAM WORDSWORTH

At times it seems that the only thing we can count on are the cycles of the seasons. No matter what else happens, we know that the surge of new life at springtime will give way to the full-blown beauty of summer. The ripe autumn harvest welcomes winter as nature prepares once again for a fresh new start.

Many a sage has looked to the cycles of nature to understand the cycles of the soul. "Even the seasons form a great circle in their changing, and always come back again to where they were. The life of a man is a circle from childhood to childhood and so it is in everything where power moves," said the Sioux holy man Black Elk. French philosopher and author Voltaire put it this way, "It is not more surprising to be born twice than once; everything in nature is resurrection."

Karma and reincarnation tell us that our soul, following the patterns of nature, journeys along a path of birth, maturation, death and then the renewed opportunity of rebirth. They tell us that we are a part of a moving stream of consciousness and that through many life experiences our soul is evolving. Karma and reincarnation explain that our soul, like the legendary phoenix, does indeed rise from the ashes of our former selves to be reborn and that our former lives contain the seeds of our new life. In other words, everything we are today we have been building for thousands of years.

The natural cycles of karma and reincarnation can help us understand how we got where we are today and what we can do about it. They can help us understand why we were born with a particular set of aptitudes and talents, crises and challenges, assignments and aspirations. They can help us deal with the questions that tease us in moments of

One of the most ancient symbols of rebirth, rejuvenation and immortality is the phoenix. The phoenix legend, in various forms, appears in ancient Egypt, Greece, China, Japan, Ireland, Turkey,  Persia and also in Christian writings.

According to the legends, the phoenix is the only one of its kind. When its lifetime comes to a close—every five hundred years—it builds itself a nest of spices. The nest is ignited by the sun or by the phoenix itself as it fans its wings, and the bird is consumed by the conflagration. Out of its ashes a young and vibrant phoenix arises. One version of the legend explains that out of the ashes a single glowing spark remains, representing the immortal spirit, from which new life is kindled.

In spiritual terms, the rebirth of the phoenix out of the fiery flames portends both the testing and the reincarnation of the soul. Through the sometimes fiery trials and traumas of life, the soul is purified and refined, ascending to higher and higher levels of consciousness.

exasperation—*Why was I born to these parents? Why did I give birth to the children I have? Why am I afraid of the water or of heights? Why am I here?*

In this book we'll talk about the underlying principles as well as the practical aspects of karma and reincarnation: How the belief in reincarnation spans East and West, through many centuries and cultures. Why karma is the x factor in our relationships, our health, our career—every aspect of our life. Why karma *isn't* fate. How karma works. How we can trace the karmic threads we have woven from lifetime to lifetime.

We'll also talk about the traps that keep us from working through our karma and taking full advantage of our rites of passage. Finally, we'll share some tools and techniques that can help you transform karmic encounters into grand opportunities to shape the future you want. Whether or not you believe in reincarnation and karma, this book will offer new ways of thinking about life's most profound paradoxes—and promises.

PART 1

Karmic Truths

*I had the feeling that I was a historical fragment,
an excerpt for which the preceding and succeeding
text was missing.... I could well imagine that I might
have lived in former centuries and there encountered
questions I was not yet able to answer; that I had
to be born again because I had not fulfilled
the task that was given to me.*

—CARL JUNG

The Universal Law of Love

> *Is there one maxim which ought be acted upon throughout one's whole life? Surely it is the maxim of loving-kindness: Do not unto others what you would not have them do unto you.*
> —CONFUCIUS

Karma picks up where the golden rule leaves off. Do unto others as you would have them do unto you—*because someday it will be done unto you.* The Sanskrit word *karma* means "act," "action," "word" or "deed." The law of karma as it is traditionally taught says that our thoughts, words and deeds—positive and negative—create a chain of cause and effect, and that we will personally experience the effect of every cause we have set in motion. Karma, therefore, is our greatest benefactor, returning to us the good we have sent to others. It is also our greatest teacher, allowing us to learn from our mistakes.

Because the law of karma gives back to us

whatever we have sent forth as thought, word or deed, some think of it as punishment. Not so. The law of karma is the law of love. There is no greater love than having the opportunity to understand the consequences of our action—or our inaction—so that our soul can grow. Karma teaches us to love and to love and to love as no other process can. It gives us hope.

Take, for example, the tragic case of Avianca flight 052. In 1990, after a long trip from Colombia, it was trying to land at John F. Kennedy International Airport. Controllers and bad weather had delayed its landing for an hour and seventeen minutes. The jet ran out of fuel and crashed into a hillside in Cove Neck, New York, killing seventy-three and injuring eighty-five.

The National Transportation Safety Board said that inadequate traffic flow management contributed to the accident as well as faulty communication. The crew did not communicate an emergency fuel situation, which would have enabled them to have a priority landing. The official transcript of the cockpit voice recorder shows that the first officer, who had the job of communicating with air-traffic controllers, told the control tower that the plane was low on fuel, but he never used the word *emergency* even though the pilot directed him to.

In karmic terms, the first officer was at least partially accountable for the deaths and injuries of those on board. Having died in the crash himself, how would he be able to pay his debt to the people harmed by his negligence? Would God send him to hell?

According to the law of cause and effect, the law of karma, here's one possible scenario: he will mercifully be allowed to reincarnate and have the opportunity to work in a position where he can serve those who had suffered. The passengers whose destiny in this life may have been cut short through this accident will also be given another opportunity to live and complete their soul journey.

A single lifetime, whether lived to nine or ninety-nine, is just not enough time for the soul to pay off her karmic debts, develop her vast potential or fulfill her reason for being. How could we learn all our spiritual lessons or share all our unique talents on the stage of life in only one lifetime?

A Belief without Boundaries

The most striking fact at first sight about the doctrine of the repeated incarnations of the soul ... is the constant reappearance of the faith in all parts of the world.... No other doctrine has exerted so extensive, controlling, and permanent an influence upon mankind.

—REV. WILLIAM R. ALGER

The belief in karma and reincarnation criss-crosses time and space, finding a home in many cultures, both ancient and modern. The most elaborately developed concepts of karma and reincarnation are found in the religious traditions of India, especially Hinduism, Buddhism, Jainism and Sikhism.

These traditions explain that the soul reaps both the good and the bad that she has sown in previous lifetimes. "Just as a farmer plants a certain kind of seed and gets a certain crop, so it is with good and bad deeds," explains the Mahabharata, the great Hindu epic. The Dhammapada, a collection of sayings of the Buddha, tells us: "What we are today comes from our thoughts of yesterday.... If a man speaks or acts with an impure mind, suffering follows him as the wheel of the cart follows the beast that draws the cart.... If a man speaks or acts with a pure mind, joy follows him as his own shadow."

Although this fact is unknown to many Westerners, before the advent of Christianity reincarnation was also a part of the spiritual beliefs of many of the peoples of Europe, including the early Teutonic tribes, the Finns, Icelanders, Lapps, Norwegians, Swedes, Danes, early Saxons and the Celts of Ireland, Scotland, England, Brittany, Gaul and Wales. The Welsh have even claimed that it was the Celts who originally carried the belief in reincarnation to India.

In ancient Greece, both Pythagoras and Plato believed in reincarnation. Pythagoras taught that the soul's many incarnations were opportunities for her to purify and perfect herself. Some Native Americans as well as many tribes in Central and South America have believed in reincarnation. Today the belief also exists among over one hundred tribes in Africa as well as among the Eskimos and Central Australian tribes and many peoples of the Pacific, including the Tahitians,

Melanesians and Okinawans.

What about the Judeo-Christian tradition? The law of karma, as the law of cause and effect, is firmly rooted in that tradition. According to some scholars, statements made by the first-century Jewish historian Josephus may indicate that the Pharisees and the Essenes believed in reincarnation. We know that Philo, the great Jewish philosopher and contemporary of Jesus, taught reincarnation. The third-century Church Father Origen of Alexandria noted that reincarnation was part of the mystical teachings of the Jews.

In addition, reincarnation was and is taught by students of Kabbalah, a system of Jewish mysticism that flowered in the thirteenth century and is enjoying a resurgence today. Reincarnation is also part of the religious beliefs of the Jewish Hasidic movement, founded in the eighteenth century.

Last but not least, history itself as well as ancient manuscripts unearthed in this century reveal that reincarnation was alive and well in early Christianity. As we will show, even through the thirteenth century, certain groups of Christians openly espoused reincarnation alongside traditional Christian beliefs.

Karma in the Bible

*As thou hast done, it shall be done
unto thee.*
—BOOK OF OBADIAH

*Blessed are the merciful: for they
shall obtain mercy.*
—JESUS

Although the Old Testament does not explicitly
refer to reincarnation, it is filled with stories
of karmic law exacting penalties for harmful or
devious actions and rewards for good actions. One
graphic example comes from the life of King David.
David falls in love with Bathsheba, the wife of
Uriah the Hittite, and she conceives a child by him.
David secretly assigns Uriah to the front lines of
battle, knowing that he will be killed, and then
marries Bathsheba.

The Lord then sends the prophet Nathan to tell
David that because he has slain Uriah and married
his wife, he will in turn be punished. Because God
has forgiven David, Nathan says he will not take
David's life, but the price of his sin will be the life

of the child born to Bathsheba. No different from any of us, David had to learn the consequences for taking another's life.

The testings and trials of the Israelites during forty years of wandering in the wilderness colorfully depict the boomerang of returning karma. When Moses walks down Mount Sinai with the two tablets of stone containing the law and the ten commandments written by God, he discovers that the Israelites are worshiping a golden calf they have fashioned after the gods of Egypt. Three thousand of the people are punished with death.

On another occasion, Moses' sister, Miriam, challenges her brother's authority. As a result, she is afflicted with leprosy until she is healed by Moses' intercessory prayer. When a group of Israelites rebel under the leadership of Korah, the earth splits open beneath them and swallows up them and their families.

One of the most poignant lessons of karma is experienced by Moses himself. The Israelites once again test their leader's patience as they set up camp at a place where there is no water. Why bother to bring us out of Egypt, they complain, if we are going to die here of thirst? The Lord commands

Moses to take his rod in hand and order a rock to give forth water. Moses, however, is so angry that instead of speaking to the rock, he strikes it twice with his rod. The water flows abundantly to quench the people's thirst, but Moses has disobeyed God. The karmic consequences? Tragically, he is forbidden to enter the promised land.

The same law of cause and effect taught in the Old Testament is affirmed by Jesus. The Sermon on the Mount is one of the greatest lessons on karma that you will find anywhere. In it, Jesus states the mathematical precision of the law of personal accountability: "Blessed are the merciful: for they shall obtain mercy.... Judge not, that ye be not judged. For with what judgment ye judge, ye shall be judged: and with what measure ye mete, it shall be measured to you again.... Therefore all things whatsoever ye would that men should do to you, do ye even so to them: for this is the law and the prophets."

On another occasion, Jesus teaches that we are karmically responsible for what we say: "Every idle word that men shall speak, they shall give account thereof in the day of judgment. For by thy words thou shalt be justified, and by thy words thou shalt be condemned."

At the scene of his arrest, Jesus reiterates the law of karmic retribution. One of his disciples cuts off the ear of the high priest's servant. Jesus tells his disciple to put his sword away, "for all who draw the sword will die by the sword." Jesus then compassionately heals the man's ear, blessing the servant and saving his disciple from reaping the karma of having harmed another.

The apostle Paul also sets forth the law of karma when he says, "Every man shall bear his own burden.... Be not deceived; God is not mocked: for whatsoever a man soweth, that shall he also reap.... Every man shall receive his own reward according to his own labor."

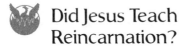 # Did Jesus Teach Reincarnation?

> *"Elijah has already come, and they did not recognize him, but they did to him whatever they pleased."... Then the disciples understood that he was speaking to them about John the Baptist.*
>
> —THE BOOK OF MATTHEW

Jesus certainly taught the concept of karma, as we have seen, but did he teach reincarnation? Both the Bible and other early Christian texts provide compelling evidence that both he and some of his followers did.

The first piece of evidence is the episode involving the man who was born blind. As Jesus and his disciples passed by the blind man, the disciples asked, "Master, who did sin, this man or his parents that he was born blind?" They were offering two possible causes for his blindness. They asked whether the blindness was a result of the parents' sin because they knew the Old Testament law that says, "The sins of the father shall be visited upon the sons to the third and fourth generation." But they also asked if the blindness was a result of the man's own sin. Since the man was *born* blind, the only way he could have sinned before his birth was to have done it in a previous lifetime.

Jesus astounded them all when he replied, "Neither hath this man sinned, nor his parents: but that the works of God should be made manifest in him."[1] The man hadn't sinned and his parents hadn't sinned. By free will, he had incarnated with this condition so that Jesus could heal him—so that the works of God could be revealed in him.

If Jesus had not believed in karma or reincarnation, this was the moment when he could have denied these doctrines, but he did not. As a matter of fact, there is no record whatsoever—either in the Gospels, the writings of the apostles, the Book of Revelation or other Christian texts—that Jesus ever denied karma or reincarnation.

In fact, this account indicates that Jesus and his disciples had ongoing talks about karma and reincarnation. Jesus didn't invalidate his disciples' question nor did he elaborate on the options they offered. It wasn't necessary for Jesus to rehearse the ABCs of what the disciples already knew. Instead, Jesus used this as an opportunity to demonstrate that there are exceptions to universal law, and this was one of them.

A second example of Jesus teaching reincarnation takes place as the disciples are walking down the Mount of Transfiguration with him. On the mountain they had seen Moses and Elijah talking with Jesus. The disciples asked Jesus, "Why do the scribes say that Elijah must come first?" In other words, if Elijah is supposed to come before you, what is he doing in heaven and why haven't we seen him yet on earth?

Jesus answered, "Elijah is indeed coming and will restore all things; but I tell you that Elijah has already come, and they did not recognize him, but they did to him whatever they pleased." The Book of Matthew follows that with the statement "Then the disciples understood that he was speaking to them about John the Baptist."[2] Jesus was revealing that Elijah had reincarnated as John the Baptist, who tragically had been imprisoned and then beheaded by Herod.

It was a popular belief among the Jews of Jesus' day that the prophet Elijah would come again as the forerunner of the Messiah, as Malachi had prophesied: "Behold, I will send you Elijah the prophet before the coming of the great and dreadful day of the Lord."

The idea that this passage implies a belief in reincarnation is not something new to this century. The fact that the fourth-century Church Father Jerome specifically argues that the passage from Matthew should *not* be interpreted as supporting reincarnation tells us that some Christians of his day believed that Jesus and the disciples accepted, or were at least aware of, the concept of reincarnation.

Some Christians say that because the Bible doesn't include comprehensive teaching on reincarnation, Christians should not believe in the idea. If one followed that rationale, Christians wouldn't believe in the doctrines of the Trinity or original sin—neither of which appear in the Bible.

We also know that not all of Jesus' original teachings have survived. The Book of Acts says that following the resurrection, Jesus taught his disciples for forty days of "things pertaining to the kingdom of God." There is no record of what he said. John closes his gospel by explicitly telling us, "There are also many other things which Jesus did, the which, if they should be written every one,

I suppose that even the world itself could not contain the books that should be written."

In addition, it is quite plausible that Jesus would have been exposed to the idea of reincarnation. In his day, Greek ideas penetrated Jewish thought and many scholars believe that Jesus, like many first-century Jews, spoke Greek and would have easily come into contact with Greek ideas. One of the currents running through the broad stream of Greek religion was a belief in reincarnation.

The Roman statesman Cicero and the great Roman poet Virgil, both of whom lived around the time of Jesus, also espoused reincarnation. Given the multicultural climate of Palestine and the trade routes stretching to the East, Jesus could also have come into contact with Indian ideas on reincarnation.[3] In addition, there is substantial evidence, which I review in my book *The Lost Years of Jesus,* that between the ages of twelve and thirty Jesus himself visited India.[4]

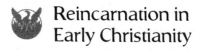# Reincarnation in Early Christianity

*Every soul ... comes into this world
strengthened by the victories or weakened
by the defeats of its previous life.*

—CHURCH FATHER ORIGEN OF ALEXANDRIA

Can you be a Christian and still believe in reincarnation? Today the majority of Christian denominations would answer no to that question. But not in the second century.

Early Christianity was extremely diverse. During the first three centuries of this new religion, the Christian community was composed of numerous sects, including several groups now known collectively as Gnostics. The Gnostics claimed to possess an advanced teaching that had been secretly handed down to them from Jesus through his closest disciples. Even among the Gnostics, there were differences in beliefs and practices. Some were strictly ascetic; others were accused of being morally licentious. Some were celibate; others were not. But they did share some common beliefs.

They believed that the means to salvation was not simply through faith, as the emerging orthodox contingent claimed, but through *gnosis*— a Greek word meaning "knowledge" or "acquaintance." The Gnostics emphasized a personal knowledge and experience of the Divine. They believed that the quest for self-knowledge would lead to reintegration with the divine Self that is the essence of our identity. To the Gnostics, karma and reincarnation created the context for that mystical union.

In the Gnostic *Book of Thomas,* probably written toward the end of the second century, Jesus teaches that after death some will remain consumed "in their concern about life" and "will be brought back to the visible realm." Toward the end of this work, Jesus says, "Watch and pray that you may not be born in the flesh, but that you may leave the bitter bondage of this life."[5] In other words, pray that you are not reborn on earth but that you return to higher realms.

In another Gnostic text, *Pistis Sophia,* probably written in the third century, Jesus describes various karmic consequences for actions taken in previous lives. He says that a person will be "cast back into the world again according to the type of the sins which he hath committed." A person who is a "curser," for example, will be "continually troubled" in his heart. The soul of one who is "arrogant and overweening" will be cast "into a lame and deformed body, so that all despise it persistently." Someone who has not sinned but who has not yet received the mysteries of the spiritual world will be placed in a body that will enable him to "find the signs of the mysteries of the Light and inherit the Light-kingdom forever."[6]

In addition to the Gnostics, in the second and third centuries many prominent Christians accepted reincarnation. Clement of Alexandria, a Christian teacher who headed the Church's catechetical school in Alexandria, is said to have been one of them. His successor, Origen of Alexandria—a Church Father and the most influential theologian of the Greek Church—believed in the preexistence of the soul, if not reincarnation.

Origen's *On First Principles* explains that souls are assigned to their "place or region or condition" based on their actions "before the present life." God has "arranged the universe on the principle of a most impartial retribution," he tells us.[7]

God didn't create "from any favoritism" but gave souls bodies "according to the sin of each."[8]

"If souls did not pre-exist," asks Origen, "why is it that we find some blind from their birth, having done no sin, while others are born having nothing wrong with them?"[9] He answers his own question: "It is clear that certain sins existed [i.e., were committed] before the souls [came into bodies], and as a result of these sins each soul receives a recompense in proportion to its deserts."[10] In other words, people's fates are based on their past actions.

Origen's belief in the preexistence of the soul implies reincarnation. For this, his followers and his teachings were later attacked in the controversial crossfire of ecclesiastical canon. Three centuries after Origen's death, the Byzantine emperor Justinian declared Origen a heretic. At the emperor's instigation, a Church council anathematized ("cursed") Origen's teaching on the preexistence of the soul. Origenist monks were expelled and Origen's writings destroyed.

Since there are no records documenting papal approval of these anathemas, scholars today question their legitimacy. But the council's action, accepted in practice by the Church, made reincarnation incompatible with Christianity. Between the third and sixth centuries, the authorities of Church and State gradually rejected Christians who believed in reincarnation, banning and finally destroying their manuscripts.

From time to time, belief in reincarnation did stubbornly resurface. It traveled to the areas of present-day Bosnia and Bulgaria, appearing in the seventh century with the Paulicians and in the tenth century with the Bogomils. Reincarnation beliefs showed up in medieval France and Italy, where they formed a central part of the Cathar sect.

The dread Inquisition was originally established in the thirteenth century to combat the Cathars, also known as the Albigenses. The Church finally won the battle by waging a crusade followed by a brutal campaign of inquisition, torture and burnings.

At that point, belief in reincarnation went underground. It was kept alive through the nineteenth century in the secret traditions of the alchemists, Rosicrucians, Kabbalists, Hermeticists and Freemasons. Reincarnation continued to crop up inside the Church as well. In nineteenth-century

Poland, for instance, a Catholic archbishop, Monsignor Passavalli (1820–97), grafted reincarnation onto his faith and openly embraced it. He influenced other Polish and Italian priests, who also took up reincarnation.[11]

 West Meets East

I believe I shall, in some shape or other, always exist, and, with all the inconveniences human life is liable to, I shall not object to a new edition of mine, hoping, however, that the errata of the last may be corrected.

—BENJAMIN FRANKLIN

Even though early Christians and perhaps even Jesus himself had espoused reincarnation, Church councils effectively inoculated Christians against the idea. As the decades and centuries rolled by, however, some Western thinkers began thinking outside the box and had to admit that reincarnation made at least as much sense as a doctrine of a one-shot chance before heaven or hell.

A man with no less stature and genius than the twentieth-century philosopher, physician and missionary Albert Schweitzer once said that "reincarnation contains a most comforting explanation of reality by means of which Indian thought surmounts difficulties which baffle the thinkers of Europe."[12] As nineteenth-century German philosopher Arthur Schopenhauer put it, "Were an Asiatic to ask me for a definition of Europe, I should be forced to answer him: It is that part of the world which is haunted by the incredible delusion that man was created out of nothing, and that his present birth is his first entrance into life."[13]

The contrast between East and West was described quite bluntly, and humorously, by a nine-year-old Hindu boy who wrote in a school essay about the cat, his favorite animal: "The cat has four legs, one in each corner. He also has nine lives, which he does not use in Europe because of Christianity."[14]

What many Westerners don't realize is that some of the greatest thinkers in the West, past and present, have embraced reincarnation. The concept made a lot of sense to American founding father Benjamin Franklin, for example. At the age of twenty-two, he wrote an epitaph for himself, although it wasn't used when he died. It read in part, "The body of B. Franklin, printer, like the cover of an old book, its contents torn out . . . lies here food for worms, but the work shall not be lost, for it will as he believed appear once more in a new and more elegant edition revised and corrected by the author."

Years later, at the age of seventy-nine, Franklin wrote in a letter, "When I see nothing annihilated (in the works of God) and not a drop of water wasted, I cannot suspect the annihilation of souls, or believe that He will suffer the daily waste of millions of minds ready-made that now exist, and put himself to the continual trouble of making new ones."[15]

The list of other prominent Westerners who have accepted or thought seriously about reincarnation in recent centuries is long and impressive. In addition to those we have already cited, it includes such eighteenth- and nineteenth-century greats as French philosopher Voltaire, German poet Johann Wolfgang von Goethe, French novelist Honoré de Balzac, American transcendentalist and essayist Ralph Waldo Emerson, American poet Henry Wadsworth Longfellow and American industrialist

Henry Ford. From the twentieth century, the list includes British novelist Aldous Huxley, Irish poet W. B. Yeats, British author Rudyard Kipling, Finnish composer Jean Sibelius, Spanish painter Salvador Dali and American general George S. Patton.

Among those who have written about reincarnation or had their characters express reincarnationist ideas are British poets William Wordsworth and Percy Bysshe Shelley, German poet Friedrich Schiller, French novelist Victor Hugo, Swiss psychiatrist Carl Jung and American authors J. D. Salinger and Jack London.[16]

Today, belief in reincarnation is on the rise. Millions of Americans, Europeans and Canadians believe in reincarnation. By conservative estimates, over one-fifth of American adults believe in reincarnation—including a fifth of all Christians. The figures are similar for Europe and Canada. Another 22 percent of Americans say they are "not sure" about reincarnation, indicating that they are at least open to the idea. The rise in accounts of near-death experiences and past-life recollections has contributed to the acceptance of reincarnation.

Compelling Evidence

The evidence for reincarnation, although mostly circumstantial, is now so compelling that intellectual assent is natural.... We've lived before in past lives and will likely live again in future lives.

—DR. JOEL L. WHITTON

Apart from the religious and philosophical reflections about reincarnation, there is a growing body of research on the subject. For some of the most prominent voices in the field, the evidence surfaced unexpectedly, forcing them to change their perspective about life and death.

Twentieth century American clairvoyant Edgar Cayce, known as the Sleeping Prophet, was shocked the first time one of his "readings" talked about reincarnation. For twenty years, Cayce had been giving medical readings, which he dictated to a secretary while in a trancelike sleep. Through his unique gift, he dispensed medical diagnoses and described natural remedies that healed many who came to him for help. He could even successfully

diagnose patients long-distance with only a name
and address in hand.

As a devout and orthodox Christian, Cayce
never entertained the idea of reincarnation—until,
to his utter surprise, one of the readings talked
about the past life of his subject. Eventually, after
much soul searching, Cayce came to accept the
idea of reincarnation as compatible with Jesus'
teachings. More than twenty-five hundred people
learned about their past lives through Cayce's work.
He revealed how their interactions in past incarnations had determined the course of their present
life. In many cases, he told them how karmic patterns woven through lifetimes had resulted in their
emotional or physical afflictions.

Rabbi Yonassan Gershom in his book *Beyond
the Ashes* describes how evidence for reincarnation
came to him unexpectedly. Over a period of ten
years 250 people, both Jews and non-Jews, came
to him for counseling because they had flashbacks,
spontaneous memories, dreams and visions of
having died in the Holocaust in a past life.

Some of the evidence for reincarnation comes
from those who have recalled past lives under
hypnosis. Although I do not recommend hypnosis

as a tool in therapy or for delving into past lives,* the findings from past-life regressions are interesting and they often confirm the teachings on reincarnation and the afterlife that have come down to us through various spiritual traditions. Dr. Alexander Cannon says he did his best to disprove reincarnation and even told his trance subjects that their memories were nonsense. "Yet as the years went by one subject after another told me the same story in spite of different and varied conscious beliefs," he wrote in 1950. "Now well over a thousand cases have been so investigated and I have to admit that there is such a thing as reincarnation."[17]

Dr. Helen Wambach, the clinical psychologist and regression therapy expert who pioneered past-life and prenatal research, regressed hundreds of people in the course of her career. She once said, "Ninety percent of the people who come to me definitely flash on images from a past life."

Dr. Morris Netherton, a regression therapist since the 1960s, had a healing experience that

*Hypnosis, even when done with the best of intentions, can make us spiritually vulnerable. It can open us to elements of the subconscious and unconscious of the practitioner. Through hypnosis we may also prematurely uncover records of events from past lives that we are not ready to deal with (see pages 111–14).

changed his beliefs about reincarnation. Raised a fundamental southern Methodist, he hadn't thought much about past lives. At the time he was undergoing conventional therapy to ease a number of problems including a chronic ulcer. "In the third session I talked about the pain I was feeling," he writes, "and the next thing I knew I was in a different place."[18] He saw himself in an institution for the criminally insane in the early 1800s, where a sentry kicked him in the stomach, in the exact place of the ulcer. The pain, he says, immediately subsided and never returned.

Whether this past-life incident had really happened or was metaphorical, it dramatically changed Netherton's direction—he went on to found an institute that teaches regression therapy.

Most reincarnation accounts have not been able to provide details that can be checked against historical sources. A recent and intriguing testimony by an unlikely candidate does just that. In 1999, Captain Robert L. Snow, commander of the homicide branch of the Indianapolis Police Department, published the story of his search for a past life in a book called *Looking for Carroll Beckwith*.

Raised in a strict Methodist family and working in the no-nonsense police profession, Snow never toyed with the idea of reincarnation. He thought it only was for "kooks and weirdos." Then one day at a party, he told a child-abuse detective who used hypnotic regression therapy that past-life regression was probably based on a lot of imagination. "Besides," he said, "if it was true, then how come no one's ever proved they've lived a past life?"[19]

That's when the detective, a woman, politely challenged him to test his beliefs. She wrote down the name of a colleague who used hypnotic regression. Snow reluctantly took on her dare and under hypnosis he recalled, among other things, a past life as an artist. He saw his studio and some of the paintings he had created in that lifetime. At first Snow dismissed the session as a product of his subconscious mind. In true detective style, he decided to prove to himself that he had simply patched together memories of paintings he had seen before in a history or art book.

His search, however, proved just the opposite. First he couldn't find a picture of the paintings anywhere in a book. Then, in a small art gallery in New Orleans, he stumbled across the *exact* portrait he had seen himself painting under hypnosis.

It was a rare work by a not-so-famous artist that had been in a private collection, so there was no chance he had ever seen it on display or in a book. Once he found out the name of the artist, J. Carroll Beckwith, he was off and running.

Rummaging through diaries, scrapbooks and biographies, he went on to prove twenty-eight details that he remembered in regression—including that he had been upset about poor lighting for one of his paintings, he had painted a portrait of a woman with a hunchback, he didn't like painting portraits but needed the money, his paintings were full of sun and bright colors, and he had died in the fall of the year in a big city.

"I have uncovered evidence that proves beyond a doubt the existence of a past life," writes Snow in his fascinating account. "The evidence I uncovered in this two-year investigation is so overwhelming that if it had been a criminal case, there would be no plea bargaining. A conviction would be assured.... What this all means, however, in the bigger picture of the other billions of inhabitants of Earth, I will leave to the philosophers and theologians."[20]

Out of the Mouth of Babes

*Mere children... grasp innumerable facts
with such speed as to show that they are
not then taking them in for the first time,
but remembering and recalling them.*

—CICERO

Some of the most compelling evidence for reincarnation comes from children. Dr. Ian Stevenson, the world's foremost investigator of children's past-life memories, prefers not to deal with hypnosis. Instead he interviews children who have had spontaneous past-life memories and then tries to independently verify the details of their previous existence. Stevenson, a psychiatrist, has meticulously documented twenty-five hundred of these cases, chiefly from India, Sri Lanka and Burma.

One of the most remarkable and best-documented cases of reincarnation is that of Shanti Devi from India. Mohandas Gandhi appointed a committee of fifteen people to study her unusual case. At three years of age, Shanti began speaking about her husband and children from her past life. Eventually she told her new family her husband's name and the name of the town eighty miles away where they had lived. She described how her husband looked and how she had died after giving birth to her second child. A relative of her husband's was sent to investigate and Shanti recognized him on his arrival. She described the house she had lived in and even told him where she had buried some money—a fact that her husband later verified.

When her husband came to see her unannounced, she immediately recognized him. Shanti finally led the committee of investigators to her previous home. She used idioms of speech familiar in that town, although she had never been there before, and recognized her husband's brother and father.

I have found that children do have past-life memories until about age three. They don't necessarily understand what they are seeing and they may or may not be able to clearly articulate it. Recently a two-year-old I know was looking at a book that showed a woman baking. When her sitter asked, "Did you ever bake a cake?" the toddler replied, "Oh, yes. Not now. Before. Before I grew into a baby."

Helen Wambach in her book *Reliving Past Lives* tells how a five-year-old youngster named Peter, whom she was treating for hyperactivity, one day began telling her of his life as a rookie policeman. He told her that he liked to smoke and didn't know why he couldn't smoke now. He also said he had played basketball.

During the course of his treatment, Peter remained hyperactive but he was able to sit and relax when he talked about his life as a policeman. "The subject seemed to obsess him," wrote Wambach. "One day his mother reported that a policeman had brought him home because he was out in the middle of the street trying to direct traffic."[21]

A parent who believes in reincarnation sent me this account of her daughter's past-life memory: "When my daughter was two years and ten months old, she had an interesting past-life memory while attending a family reunion with many relatives whom she had never seen before. She remembered being the person of her own great-great-grandmother, whose name was Gertrude.

"First my daughter saw a picture of Gertrude at age twenty on the wall and with a puzzled look she said, 'Is that me?' The next day while playing peekaboo with her great-great-uncle (Gertrude's son), she suddenly stopped her playing and out of the blue she said, 'Am I your mother?'

"That evening while watching slides, there was projected on the screen a picture of myself at age five standing next to my great-great grandmother, Gertrude, who was seated beside me. My daughter began to shout, 'Mama, that's me! that's me!' I replied, 'No dear, that's a picture of me when I was a little girl.' My daughter responded emphatically, 'No, the one sitting down!'

"The next day my daughter saw my cousin who is believed to be a reembodiment of Gertrude's husband and she asked him, 'Are you my daddy?' (At that time, she used the term *daddy* to mean husband.) After returning home some days after the family reunion, my daughter looked up from her coloring and said, 'Mama, my name is Gertie, call me Gertie,' then resumed her coloring. (Gertrude was indeed called Gertie in that life.)

"All this happened over five years ago and my daughter has since forgotten these memories, but this has given me insight into her mission in this life. Gertrude was a conservative Protestant, well-versed in the Bible, who taught Sunday School for over forty years. In the 1930s, Gertrude's daughter joined the Theosophical Society, which espoused reincarnation. This was a great shock and embarrassment to Gertrude. She could never accept these 'strange Eastern teachings' but vowed that when she got to heaven she would ask Jesus for the truth! Jesus, in his great mercy, has allowed my daughter to reembody into a family situation where she can learn that truth."

At about four years old, I had my own past-life memory. I was playing in my sandbox in the picket-fenced play yard my father had built for me. I was alone, enjoying myself in the sun, watching the sand slip through my little fingers.

Then all of a sudden, as though someone had turned the dial on a radio, I was on another frequency—playing in the sand along the Nile River in Egypt. It was just as real as my play yard in Red Bank, New Jersey, and just as familiar. I was idling away the hours, splashing in the water and feeling the warm sand on my body. My Egyptian mother was nearby. Somehow this, too, was my world. I had known that river forever.

How did I know it was Egypt and the Nile? My parents had put up a map of the world over my toy chest and I already knew the names of the countries. My parents were both world travelers and my mother would tell me stories about the countries.

So after some time (I don't know how much time had passed), it was as though the dial turned again and I was back at home in my little play yard. I wasn't dizzy. I wasn't dazed. I was back to the present, very much aware that I had been somewhere else.

I jumped up and ran to find my mother. I found her at the kitchen stove and I blurted out my story. "What happened?" I asked. She sat me down and looked at me and said, "You have remembered a past life." With those words she opened another dimension.

Instead of ridiculing or denying what I had experienced, she spoke to me in terms a child could understand: "Our body is like a coat we wear. It gets worn out before we finish what we have to do. So God gives us a new mommy and a new daddy and we are born again so we can finish the work God sent us to do and finally return to our home of light in heaven. Even though we get a new body, we still have the same soul. And our soul remembers the past, even though our mind may not."

As she spoke, I felt as if she was reawakening my soul memory. It was as though I had always known these things. I told her that I knew I had lived forever. Over the years she was to point out to me children who were born maimed and others who were gifted, some who were born into wealthy homes and others into poverty. She believed that their past actions had led to their present circumstances. She said that there could be no such thing as divine or human justice if we only had one life. We could only know God's justice if we could experience the consequences of our past actions returning to us in our present life.

I was very comfortable in the awareness that I had lived before. Fortunately, I did not have anyone near me who denied this gentle experience and the tender musings of my soul.

Although you may not have had a memory of a past life, you've probably had the sense of being familiar with a person or place on first contact. Perhaps it was meeting someone for the first time and feeling that you were already old friends, or having an instantaneous and inexplicable loathing for someone who just walked into the room.

There is a good reason why we don't usually remember our past. God pulls down the shade, so to speak, when we enter the birth canal. This curtain of forgetfulness is an act of mercy. We have an assignment for this life and we can't really focus on more than one life at a time and make a go of it.

Now and then God may show us a frame or two from a previous life episode. When we are allowed to take a peek at our karmic book of life, it is for a purpose. It may be to quicken our souls to remember the commitments we made before coming into embodiment. Perhaps we need to understand the underlying cause of a negative episode from the past so we can have compassion, forgive and move on. But it's not essential to know all about our past lives in order to deal with our karma and make spiritual progress, and we shouldn't force it. If God wants us to know, he will show us, one way or another.

The Great Creative Plan

Our birth is but a sleep and a forgetting:
The Soul that rises with us, our life's Star,
Hath had elsewhere its setting,
And cometh from afar.

—WILLIAM WORDSWORTH

In the beginning, our soul was endowed with a unique and precious gift that we were meant to give to humanity throughout our incarnations. We were told that without that gift, the full flowering of our families, our communities and even our civilization would not take place.

Through the process of incarnating on earth, we were also meant to evolve spiritually—to grow in spiritual mastery as we nurtured our divine gifts and developed our talents. God gave us free will so that we could lovingly affirm our calling to be co-creators with the Divine. Some of us even volunteered to embody on earth, angels in disguise, to rescue those who had come before us and had forgotten that they too had a divine plan and a mission. We knew that when we had fulfilled our reason for being, we would joyfully return to realms of Spirit to continue our soul's adventure.

Our souls began the journey full of hope. We understood the true nature of our destiny. We knew that, above all else, we were spiritual beings charged with a mission to keep that spiritual consciousness alive on earth.

Somewhere along the line, we strayed from that path. We "fell" from that higher consciousness as the allure of the outer, human self and its trappings pulled our attention away from our innate, divine Self. We became self-centered rather than Self-centered, and slowly we began to forget the reason for our sojourn on earth.

The rest is history. Centered in our human ego rather than in the heart of our Higher Self, we were prompted to act in ways that did not always honor our inner spirit. We did a great many good things, but we also created negativity. Out of the misdirected need to protect the lesser self, we harmed rather than helped others. Then, by the law of the circle, we were not free to move on until we had paid off the karmic debts we now owed to others.

So now our soul's reason for being is not only to fulfill our original divine plan but also to balance our karmic ledger. Our soul, seeking resolution, is compelled to revisit those karmic encounters lifetime after lifetime until we find that resolution.

Earth, then, is like a schoolroom. We return again and again to take our lessons. Sometimes we learn from wise teachers, but in many cases our most important tutor is our karma—the positive and negative consequences of our freewill choices. When we learn all our lessons, complete all our assignments and prove our self-mastery, we will graduate from earth's schoolroom and continue our soul journey in other realms as masterful spiritual beings.

So often in today's world, wealth and physical comfort are considered to be the hallmark of success. When we look at life from a spiritual perspective, we see that our priority is not material success, although it is a legitimate tool to help us fulfill our life's purpose. Instead, we see that God's priority for us is to get back into alignment with our original blueprint—to replace the human matrix, the misguided patterns of the human ego, with our divine matrix.

Once we recognize why we are here and how we got where we are today, the paradoxes of life become much more significant—and manageable.

Once we see our life not as an isolated segment in time but as part of a continuum, our perspective changes. Once we see every today as part of the larger creative plan for our soul, our daily choices take on new meaning.

 ## An Energy Equation

The whole of what we know is a system of compensations. Each suffering is rewarded; each sacrifice is made up; every debt is paid.
—RALPH WALDO EMERSON

Let's turn from the big picture to the spiritual dynamics of everyday life. The law of karma is a precise and scientific equation of energy. The sages and mystics of East and West tell us that all of life is energy. The life coursing through our veins, our minds and our hearts is energy. Each moment the crystal clear stream of life descends to us from our Source, and each moment we are deciding whether to put a positive or negative spin on it.

By the universal law of cause and effect, that

energy will return to us. When the energy with our positive spin returns to us, we see and feel positive things come into our life. We may be surrounded by love and encouragement, have a sense of joy and the abundant life, or feel that we are making progress.

The energy that we have given a negative spin will also return to us. Perhaps we will be on the receiving end of the same kind of selfish act or harsh word we sent forth. Maybe we will find ourselves in a situation where we must give of ourselves to those we have ignored in the past. Whatever the case, we will once again have the opportunity to make the choice: Will we put a positive or a negative spin on our thoughts, our words and our deeds?

One of the key lessons we learn on the path of karma is that it is not the circumstances we find ourselves in that matter but how we react to them. Sometimes it takes a while for us to catch on. Remember the movie *Groundhog Day*? An obnoxiously egotistical TV weatherman (played by Bill Murray) sent to cover Groundhog Day in Punxsutawney, Pennsylvania, wakes up every morning to find himself at the beginning of the same day—

day after day after day. Not until he learns to transform his self-centeredness into compassion, develop
his talents and open his heart does he get the girl,
get off the merry-go-round and begin a new day.

The movie is a clever parable for life itself.
The same scenarios do play themselves out over
and over again. We meet the same characters lifetime after lifetime until we resolve to master our
negative reactions and take advantage of the opportunity staring us in the face right now to love
and love and love again.

My teacher and late husband, Mark L.
Prophet, shared this karmic truth with a man who
was bitterly unhappy with his lot. The only way he
could support his large family was in the insurance
business, but he hated his job with a passion. He
felt trapped, and as a result he was always dis-
gruntled and discordant. Master your consciousness where you are, Mark advised him, and you
will automatically evolve into a better situation
when your soul is ready. Instead, he blamed others
for his problems, looking for the answers outside
of himself. Eventually he became so unhappy that
he divorced his wife, thereby losing an opportunity
for greater self-mastery.

This isn't to say that we should never look for better job opportunities or that we will never grow out of our present circumstances or relationships. The lesson is that when our karma does compel us to stay where we are for a time, life could be sending us a message: there is something here you must master before you can move on.

 ## Karmic Consequences

God'll send the bill to you.
—JAMES RUSSELL LOWELL

Negative karma is like a speed bump. It makes us slow down and pay attention. Sometimes it's more like a roadblock, demanding that we back up and find another way of getting where we want to go or even making us think twice about our destination. Where we may have shut our eyes or closed our hearts in the past, karma asks us to open up to new possibilities.

Returning karma manifests itself in an infinite variety of ways tailored to the unique needs of our soul. It determines the families we are born into, our relationships, our careers and our health. It shapes our physical, mental, emotional and spiritual temperaments as well as the challenges we must meet.

If, for instance, we were born with a problem in our throat, in a past life we may have misused our throat—perhaps through speech that was harmful, misleading or inaccurate. Maybe we stifled another's freedom of expression and we now have to experience how that feels. If we have deliberately or indirectly caused someone's death in a past life, karmic law may now require us to give birth to that person or lend him extraordinary support.

Mark Prophet once gave this interesting example. Say a woman becomes hypercritical of her daughter-in-law. She becomes so obsessed about her that all she can talk about is how terrible this girl is. The woman, in effect, has a split. The honest part of her knows that what she is saying about her daughter-in-law has no foundation in fact, but the ego is obsessed with purveying this falsehood. Mark said that in the woman's next lifetime, this split could manifest as schizophrenia.

This, of course, does not mean that schizophrenia always has the same cause. Not at all. Because of the complexity of our past choices, no two people's karmic portrait is exactly the same.*

Edgar Cayce's readings are a fascinating study in the precision of returning karma. One of the readings traced a young man's anemic condition to a lifetime in Peru where he had seized power. "Much blood was shed," the reading said, "hence anemia in the present." A man with digestive problems had been a glutton centuries ago as an escort to King Louis XIII and was therefore now forced to eat a restricted diet. Cayce once advised a deaf person who had spent a past life as a nobleman during the French Revolution, "Do not close your ears again to those who plead for aid."

In another reading, a pretty but overweight young woman was told she had been a beautiful athlete in Roman times. She learned that in that incarnation she had ridiculed those who were less agile than she because they were heavy. A movie

---

*There are many variables in the cause-effect sequences that manifest as physical, mental and emotional conditions. The examples we share in this book are intended to help you understand how karma works, but they cannot be extrapolated to apply to all similar situations. Each karmic circumstance and its result are unique.

producer who limped as a result of developing polio as a teenager was told that when he was a Roman soldier he had jeered at those who were afraid. The reading said, "The breaking of the body this time was an experience necessary for the awakening of the inner self, and the development of spiritual forces." In one reading, Cayce articulated the bottom line: "*What you condemn in another, that you become in yourself.*"[22]

Just because we are born with a karmic condition, it does not mean that we cannot be healed of it. Sometimes the karma at the core of an illness is simply due to mistreatment of our bodies. By not taking care of the precious instrument God gave us for our spiritual evolution, we can reap the karma of neglect. If the condition is caught in time and we learn the lesson, we may recover. When our burdens have deeper causes, it may take more time and effort to balance the karma. Each case is different. We may have to bear our burden for a time so that our soul can learn a particular lesson. When we have expiated that underlying karma, we can then be liberated from the condition.

A major spiritual key to healing is not to seek healing merely for the sake of physical healing but to seek healing for the sake of wholeness—body, mind and soul. The roots of our physical illness usually reach into other dimensions of our being that need to be healed first. Once a man who had been stricken by multiple sclerosis received a reading from Cayce that showed he had "indulged his negative passions to excess" in a past incarnation. Cayce told the man that he was at war with himself and encouraged him to trust in God. Saturated with bitterness and self-pity, the man was incensed that Cayce had failed to cure him.

A subsequent reading for the same man stated that his condition was karmic. It said he would have to have a change of heart, a change of purpose and a change of intent before he would respond to healing treatments. The reading bluntly advised, "As long as there are hate, malice, injustice—those things which are at variance to patience, long suffering, brotherly love—there cannot be a healing of this body. What would the body be healed for? That it might gratify its own physical desires and appetites? That it might add to its own selfishness? Then, if so, it had better remain as is."[23]

The Roots of Our Genius

Genius is experience. Some seem to think that it is a gift or talent, but it is the fruit of long experience in many lives.

—HENRY FORD

What about the good karma we reap? What does that look like? The Dhammapada tells us that just as a man who has been far away for a long time is welcomed home with joy, so "the good works of a man in his life welcome him in another life, with the joy of a friend meeting a friend on his return."

Whereas negative karma is like a stormy sea that batters our boat from all sides, good karma is like the fair wind in our sails that effortlessly propels us forward. Whereas our accumulated negative karma keeps us tied down to the level where we made that karma, our accumulated good karma is like a magnet pulling us up into our higher consciousness.

While our negative karma represents our debts to others, our good karma is like having money in our cosmic bank account. It's a reserve we can build on. We can use our good karma—our strengths and positive momentums—to help us overcome and move beyond our negatives.

Good karma can manifest as everything from a supportive circle of family and friends to genius and talent. Our gifts and aptitudes are the seeds of our good karma bearing fruit. Our good karma and our momentums can also launch us like a rocket ship on the pathway of our soul's passion.

World War II hero General George Patton, for instance, saw himself as a leader of men in battle from the time he was a youngster. He later came to believe that he had been embodied as a warrior many times, including at Troy, with Caesar and with the Highlanders. When he took over his first command in France at Langres, a town he had never visited before, he had a déjà vu experience that added to his conviction. He told the French liaison officer who offered to show him around, "You don't have to. I know this place. I know it well."

He then told the driver where to go in the small city "almost as if someone were at my ear, whispering the directions." He directed him to what had been the Roman amphitheater, the drill ground, the Temples of Mars and Apollo. "I even showed him correctly the spot where Caesar had earlier pitched his tent," said Patton. "But I never made a wrong turn. You see, I had been there before."[24]

Singer Risë Stevens had her own déjà vu experience while she was performing in Greece. As she was singing Orpheo's aria of lamentation at the foot of the Acropolis, the scene bathed in moonlight, she "lost all touch with reality" and felt herself in ancient Greece, "mentally and physically" living a former life in which she had acted on that very stage. Later she wrote about the incident, saying she finished the aria as in a trance and fell prostrate on the body of Euridice. It took five minutes of thunderous applause to bring her back to the present.[25]

Reincarnation is the only logical explanation for childhood geniuses like Mozart, who at five wrote minuets and by nine had written sonatas, arias and symphonies. The less-known Tom Wiggins is another example. A blind and autistic child of nineteenth-century Georgian slaves, he could learn in just a few hours skills that other musicians had taken years to master.

At three, Tom could imitate piano pieces he heard being practiced in his slave-owner's home. At eight, he began a long career on the concert circuit, where he would perform classics and reproduce any piece of music that a challenger would perform first. In the middle of his performance, he would even turn around, face the audience and continue playing the piece with his hands behind his back!

Unfortunately, Tom's performances were publicized as a kind of freak show. Yet his abilities were anything but freakish. As with other child prodigies, the only sensible explanation for his extraordinary talent is that it came from attainment he had earned in past lives.

PART 2

Karmic Threads

*If you want to know the past,
look at your present life. If you want
to know the future, look at your present.*

—GAUTAMA BUDDHA

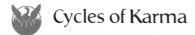 Cycles of Karma

*Karma, or cosmic justice, puts everyone
into conditions where they can either
learn or atone for something.*

—HELENA ROERICH

We have all had days when we think, "This is going to be a great day," and then the unexpected interruptions—or eruptions—begin. One day we get up and feel great and another we feel weighed down for seemingly no reason at all.

The differences in how we feel and how easily we navigate through our day have more to do with the amount and kind of karma we are dealing with than we realize. When a certain karma comes due, things suddenly change. We go to work and out of the blue our job has been cut—or we are promoted. Our test results come back and we find out that we have to go into the hospital—or that we're having twins.

Every morning the bundle of karma we have been assigned for the day greets us at our doorstep.

We are allotted a portion of good karma based on the loving, comforting and enlightening things we have done in the past. Every day a certain portion of our negative karma also arrives for resolution.

In most cases, at the age of twelve, when we are about to enter puberty, an increment of our karma from previous lifetimes descends for the first time. (Some souls volunteer to have more of their karma descend at an earlier age.) So a child's first twelve years can be a time when he learns about values, the law of karma and the correct use of energy. If by twelve, children can be taught that they have a purpose in life and can understand the importance of choice, it will be much easier for them to deal with the challenges that come their way and make it safely through their teenage years and beyond.

When karma returns, it is intricate and precise. Just look at the way a fire works—it races through a town, suddenly changing direction. Some homes are left standing and others are destroyed. The front page of a newspaper once showed a photo of a fire in a California neighborhood. The entire block was a pile of rubble—except one home, which stood unscathed. Unbelievable, yet believable when we understand the law of karma. Figuratively and literally, which way the wind blows is not a matter of chance or whimsy; it is the result of cycles of karma.

 ## Group Karma

No man is an island, entire of itself;
every man is a piece of the continent.

—JOHN DONNE

Karma is that irresistible force we have set in motion that brings us face-to-face with certain people, places and events. Like a giant magnet, it draws us to those we need to learn from as well as those who need to learn from us—and often they are the same people. Karma also magnetizes us to those we've had wonderful relationships with in the past so we can share the bounties of our mutual love. This kind of one-on-one connection is what we call personal karma.

Karma can also be collective. Entire families, towns, states and nations can share what is called group karma. When groups of people commit acts together as one body—or fail to act when they should—they reembody together either to work out or to reap the benefits of the karma they jointly created. They form what you could call a spiritual ecosystem.

When four people team up to commit a robbery, for example, they create group karma. When a number of people contribute to or fail to put a stop to pollution or persecution, they are jointly accountable for the harm they cause another— harm that may have far-reaching consequences. Long-standing vendettas, such as the intense and potentially explosive hostilities between the Israelis and the Palestinians or between India and Pakistan, can indicate ancient group karma between cultures.

Unresolved group karma can have daunting effects. Just as intense personal karma can at times produce severe physical consequences if we don't balance that karma before it falls due, negative group karma can have serious consequences to those who created it. Calamities that come through harsh and extraordinary weather conditions, for example, often indicate the return of collective karma.[1]

When calamity strikes, in whatever form, we

must respond with compassion to aid those who suffer and never be tempted to criticize, judge or ignore them because we believe they are receiving their karmic payback. Every one of us in our own time will face the karma we have made in this life and past lives, and we too may need support to get through our challenges.

We must also keep in mind that not everything that happens to people is the result of their karma, a topic we take up further on pages 125–29. Carrying one another's burden is part of the spiritual path, and it can be a golden opportunity to balance some of our own negative karma, make good karma and, last but not least, exercise the power of love.

People can also make positive karma that bonds them together with kindred souls. Those who have created beautiful music together or joined hands as doctors or writers in past lives may come together again to offer their gifts to humanity. I knew a family where the parents as well as every one of their seven children played the violin. They could very well have been together in past lives. The children's aptitude for violin may have been carried through their parents' genes, but the musical attainment and good karma these souls had garnered in past lives attracted them to their parents.

The peoples of every nation have some karma to resolve together, but they also have a collective genius—a particular endowment of talent that their culture can offer to the world. It has been said, and it is true, that many Americans were incarnated on the ancient continent of Atlantis, which sank beneath the ocean many thousands of years ago. Materialism, the abuse of power and the misuse of technology contributed to the decline of that advanced civilization.

Americans are facing the same tests and opportunities again. Can we wed science and spirituality so that we use our power and technological advancements to liberate rather than to control? Can we sustain a practical spirituality that educates the heart and soul as well as the mind? This time around, can we stay focused on inner values rather than worldly sophistication and intellectual knowledge devoid of the spirit?

Second Chances

Observe the opportunity.

—ECCLESIASTICUS

A dramatic example of how the threads of karma and opportunity are woven through lifetimes comes out of the pages of English history. This is a story of principle versus ambition. It is also a lesson of how karma gives us a second chance.

In 1155, when Thomas Becket was just thirty-six, Henry II appointed him chancellor of England. Becket was an energetic and skilled diplomat, statesman and soldier. He became the king's close friend and confidant, and the second most powerful man in the realm.

In 1161 Henry wanted Becket to become archbishop of Canterbury. Henry's motive was simple. By placing his friend in the highest offices of both Church and State, Henry would bypass the traditional tension between the archbishop and the king. Becket hesitated. He foresaw the inevitable conflict between the interests of the king and the interests of the Church. He finally assented when the king insisted, accepting the office as "God's hidden will."

After his consecration as archbishop, Becket adopted an austere and devout lifestyle in contrast to his former days as a lavish man of the world. Much to Henry's displeasure, Becket resigned his post as chancellor and zealously championed the cause of the Church. The relationship between the two men quickly deteriorated. Threatened with imprisonment or forced resignation, Becket fled to France. His exile lasted for over six years.

During that time, Henry challenged both Becket and the pope by having his son crowned co-regent by the archbishop of York, a right reserved to the archbishop of Canterbury. Becket then ex-communicated the bishops who had aided Henry and threatened England with an interdict that would close all the churches.

Henry finally backed down and invited Becket to return to England, where he was welcomed by enthusiastic crowds. It wasn't long, however, before the two clashed again. In a fit of rage Henry cried out, "What disloyal cowards do I have in my court, that not one will free me of this lowborn priest!" Four barons overheard the king's remarks and brutally murdered Thomas Becket in Canterbury Cathedral, four days after Christmas. His last words were, "For the name of Jesus and the defense of the Church, I embrace death."

Becket's murder shocked Christendom. His tomb swiftly became a shrine and the site of hundreds of reported miracles. Just three years after his death, he was canonized. In 1174, pressured by public opinion, Henry did penance at Becket's tomb.

In the sixteenth century the souls of Thomas and Henry were once again cast in the roles of chancellor and king of England. Once again they were given the choice to serve God's will or man's will, to champion principle or worldly power. Thomas Becket reembodied as Sir Thomas More, and Henry II as the infamous Henry VIII. Watch how precise is the opportunity based on past karma.

Starting in 1510 Henry VIII promoted Thomas More to a series of public offices. More was a lawyer, an accomplished classical scholar and a deeply religious man. He helped Henry write a statement against Martin Luther's doctrines, for which the pope rewarded Henry with the title of "Defender of the Faith."

Again Henry and Thomas became friends and the king appointed More the chancellor of England.

While chancellor, More gained a reputation as a prompt and honest judge. When the king started assuming authority over the Church and divorced Queen Catherine in opposition to Church law, More resigned. He refused to take an oath acknowledging that the offspring of Henry and his new wife would succeed to the throne because it contained a provision that challenged papal authority. For this he was imprisoned in the Tower of London.

In 1535, More was tried and convicted of high treason and then beheaded for opposing the Act of Supremacy, which declared Henry the supreme head of the Church in England. His last words echoed the sentiment voiced by Becket. He said that he died for the faith of the holy Catholic Church, "the king's good servant but God's first."

Like Becket, More was made a saint by the Church. Ironically, in 1538 Henry VIII had the shrine of Saint Thomas Becket broken to pieces. He also ordered Becket's name erased from the prayer books and prohibited any images of Becket in England. After so many centuries, he still had not forgiven Becket, just as he had not forgiven Thomas More.

Life Between Lives

I stared at the beautiful Being of Light who shimmered before me....Rather than issuing harsh judgment, the Being of Light was a friendly counsel, letting me feel for myself the pain and the pleasure I had caused others.

—DANNION BRINKLEY

Near-death experiences, past-life regressions and the accounts of those who "see" spiritual planes with their inner eye have all painted a picture of what takes place between lives. The accounts say that between embodiments we are in a heightened state of awareness, one that seems more real than life on earth.

They describe beautiful lakes and glistening cities as well as encounters with "beings of light." Dannion Brinkley, who has had three near-death experiences, was led to a "city of cathedrals" made "entirely of crystalline substance that glowed." He later found out that these were halls of learning—places "where there was no pain and knowledge flowed freely."[2]

Life Between Life by Dr. Joel Whitton and Joe

Fisher describes the experiences of those who recalled under hypnosis what they did between lifetimes. Some reported that they studied "in vast halls of learning equipped with libraries and seminar rooms." Doctors and lawyers spoke of "studying their respective disciplines during the interlife while others remember applying themselves to such subjects as 'the laws of the universe' and other metaphysical topics. Some people even tell of studying subjects that defy description because they have no earthly counterpart."[3]

The accounts also reveal that between lives we meet with a group, or board, of between three and seven spiritually advanced beings. Those who recall their encounter with this board say that these wise ones prepared them for the tasks ahead in their next life. Dr. Whitton's subjects reported that these beings are "highly advanced spiritually and may even have completed their cycle of earthly incarnations." They say that these beings intuitively know everything about those who come to them and "their role is to assist [them] in evaluating the life that has just passed and, eventually, to make recommendations concerning the next incarnation."[4]

In some spiritual traditions, this board is

known as the Karmic Board, a group of advanced beings who adjudicate karma, mercy and judgment on behalf of every soul. After each embodiment, our soul meets with the Karmic Board to review our progress in that life. Before we take incarnation again, we pass before this board to receive our assignment and karmic allotment. We are shown what family we will be born into and why, where we had difficulties in the past, who we have to settle accounts with and how we can take advantage of new opportunities to make spiritual progress. In essence, we review the plan for our upcoming life.

In *Life Between Life,* Whitton and Fisher say that this life plan, which they call our "karmic script," involves what our soul needs, not necessarily what it wants. "The karmic script often calls for renewed involvement with people who have figured, pleasantly or unpleasantly, in previous incarnations," they write. "In the words of one who felt compelled to make compensation to others: 'There are people I didn't treat too well in my last life, and I have to go back to the Earth plane again and work off that debt. This time, if they hurt me in return, I'm going to forgive them because all I really want to do is to go back home. This is home.'"[5]

Another of Dr. Whitton's subjects groaned, "Oh no—not *her* again!" when his spiritual advisors notified him that "his personal evolution would best be served by being reborn to a woman he had murdered in a previous life."[6]

After hearing one of my presentations that talked about the soul's experience before life, a woman wrote to tell me about a prebirth memory she had had many years earlier. She recalled being escorted by her Higher Self into a room that looked like a long hall. Men and women dressed in long robes were sitting at a table off to the right side of the room. "I remember standing before the man at the middle of the table. He had shoulder-length white hair and a white beard that touched the middle of his chest," she wrote.

"There was a gentle presence about him that helped me relax as he read my assignments for this life from the parchment he held in his hands. I was a very excited little girl—I could hardly wait to get started. . . . I left the room with my guide, and as I walked into a beautiful garden I began to sense that my mission might not be so easy. Uncertainties began to fill my mind. We sat down on a stone bench, which was surrounded by beautiful roses and flowers of all colors. I sat in deep contemplation, knowing that it would be only moments before I would be born to my current mother.

"I knew I was coming to help and support her, but I also had something very important to attend to when I became old enough. I turned to my guide with a concerned expression and asked, 'Will I lose what I have gained?' He clasped my hands gently in his own and said, 'It is up to you.'"

 Family Ties

Man is a knot, a web, a mesh into
which relationships are tied.
Only those relationships matter.
—ANTOINE DE SAINT-EXUPÉRY

Through our relationships, including those with our family, friends, mates, partners, bosses and coworkers, we have the greatest opportunity to resolve karma. The first karma we meet in life, and therefore often the most crucial to deal with, is karma with our parents and siblings.

We may have a lot to resolve with family members (or vice versa) or we may have close, loving ties. Maybe it's some of both. In either case, we come together as a family because there is something we must give one another. We may also have a mission together—something we are meant to do together to help, inspire or uplift others.

Sometimes the same souls reembody together in the same family but take different roles. A parent once wrote and told me this story: "At a very early age (about three years old) my daughter, Melanie,* was fascinated with my father, who had died when I was a young girl. Melanie grieved about not having met my father. She would talk about him, ask me lots of questions and want to hear stories about him. This went on for several years. At night I would have to sit with her for half an hour to help her work through this. Sometimes she would look sad and say to me, 'You know what I'm sad about.'

"The night before my second child was born, Melanie had a dream. She told me that she had seen Grandpa and that they had had a big party

_____
*The names in our stories have been changed, except for public figures.

because Grandpa was finally coming back. The following day my son was born. Since then, Melanie has not had the same sadness and doesn't talk about Grandpa like she did before."

One lesson that comes across loud and clear in reincarnation studies is that no matter what family you are born into, you alone are responsible for who and what you are today. We think we inherit our genius and our limitations from our parents' genes, but in fact we attract to us parents whose genes will fulfill the formula of our karma for this life. Cayce once told someone who asked which side of the family he had inherited the most from, "You have inherited most from yourself, not from your family! The family is only a river through which the soul flows."

Dr. Christopher Bache points out that popular Western psychology has made us think that our personality and unique traits derive from how we were treated at home. He says, "From a reincarnationist perspective, however, this gets everything backward. It puts the cart before the horse. The rule of thumb for reincarnation is: 'I do not have the problems I have in life because I have these parents, but rather I have these particular parents be-

cause I have chosen to work on these particular issues.'...

"They will recur in one form or another in
different areas of our life—in childhood relationships, in courtship, in marriage, in our career, in
our health, with our children, and with ourselves.
They will keep confronting us until we solve them,
until we break their code, until we free ourselves
from the inner programming that binds us to
them."[7]

Sometimes family members don't have karmic
debts with each other but the family's interactions
are designed to help them overcome limitations or
support each other. Two parents of a child who
had a mental disability were told by Cayce that in
a past life their child had turned his back on those
who were "disturbed in body and mind," prefer-
ring to indulge himself. Cayce's reading explained
that the parents' loving example of service in caring for their child was teaching this soul how
important it was to faithfully protect those who
depend on us.[8]

Often both parent and child are meant to
benefit from a situation that may seem tragic from
our limited perspective. Parents who once asked

Cayce if their conduct in past lives was to blame for the birth of their Down's syndrome child were told not to blame themselves and not to blame God. The reading revealed that the parents had been together on Atlantis, where they had cared for the maimed and helpless. The troubled soul of their Down's syndrome child was one of those they had helped. He came to them again, seeking their aid and compassion.

Cayce said that the couple had the opportunity to assist their child to balance his karma so he would not have to incarnate again in a deformed body. He also advised the mother that as she freely gave love and patient care, she was paving the way for the next child she was to bear. Cayce encouraged the woman, who had a suppressed desire to be a novelist, to use the lessons born of her sorrow for her writing projects.

The reading also revealed that the father needed to care for this child as part of his own spiritual growth. During the Revolutionary War, the father had been in charge of supplying a section of the army with food. One day his group stumbled into an ambush and some of them died or were mutilated. In the shock of the carnage, he angrily blamed his own officers, even though it had been an accident.

The record of this unfortunate event and his lack of forgiveness carried over into this life. Whenever he saw a cripple, it immediately triggered a sense of injustice within him. Cayce explained that in order to mend this emotional problem stemming from his past life, he needed to be forgiving and tolerant of others.[9] Thus, both father and son needed to be together for healing.

How can we ever say that there is no profit and growth to a soul in a body that has Down's syndrome or any other so-called defect? Every soul, whether in a healthy body or not, is gaining valuable experience. In addition, those who bear a physical burden may indeed be offering a much needed opportunity for spiritual growth to those who are caring for them. Our perspective is not always the soul's perspective.

Karma and Adoption

Nothing exists which escapes notice
from on high, in each and all its details.
Everything occurs for a special purpose.
—BAAL SHEM TOV

Destiny and karma bring us together with certain souls one way or another. Adoption is a good example. Under hypnosis, some of Dr. Helen Wambach's subjects who were adopted children said that being adopted was an essential part of their life plan.

Wambach wrote, "Some of them knew before they were born of the relationship they would have with the adoptive parents, and felt that they would not be able to come to them as their own genetic child but chose the method of adoption as a way to reach their parents." Her research led her to conclude that "chance and accident apparently played no part in the adoption."[10]

This puts a new light on the attitude among some today that "if you are pregnant and don't want to keep your child, you might as well abort it." From a spiritual perspective, it could very well be someone's karma or destiny to give birth to a certain child and then put her up for adoption so that she can find the parents she was meant to be with—parents who are not able to have children.

Two health-care professionals I knew, a husband and wife, once told me how troubled they were to see children being born into "underprivileged" families. On the other hand, they were also concerned about the physical and emotional traumas that sometimes plague women who have had an abortion. From their perspective, abortion was a better alternative than being born into a poor or negligent family.

I listened quietly and when they were finished talking I simply said, "All that may be true. But you're not looking at it from the child's perspective." They were silent and stunned. The child's perspective? They hadn't thought about it that way before.

From the point of view of the soul of the unborn child, the most painful and tragic consequence of abortion is that it aborts the divine plan of the soul—the special mission he or she has been waiting to fulfill, sometimes for thousands of years. Abortion also cuts short the divine plan of entire groups of souls who are tied together by their karma and cannot complete their mission because part of their "team" didn't make it into embodiment. Very often the child has karma with his parents and vice versa. Aborting the child may prevent them all from balancing their karma with each other and from fulfilling their projected life plan for that embodiment.

Taking it a step further, what about the children that those who were denied incarnation were supposed to give birth to? They have also missed their chance to take their place as adults on the world scene. The entire world community is missing individuals who were slated to play their roles on the stage of life at this moment in history.

All of us have a date with our destiny and with our karma. If we miss the date, we miss our opportunity to pay off old debts that we owe certain individuals—and we may not get that opportunity again for a long, long time.

Once these two health-care professionals started thinking about the issue from the child's point of view, they changed their perspective. In fact, they decided to have two more children of their own even though they were both in their forties, and the husband wrote a book about the spiritual and psychological consequences of abortion.

Soul Mates and Twin Flames

Love does not consist in gazing at each other,
but in looking together in the same direction.
—ANTOINE DE SAINT-EXUPÉRY

The knowledge of karma and reincarnation can teach us a lot about our relationships—some beautiful and some unpleasant but all very necessary to our soul's spiritual progress. In our later years, the relationships that usually have the most impact on our spiritual growth, for better or for worse, are our marriages.

Marriages are often woven from the intricate threads of the partners' past history together. From the perspective of past lives, there are three basic kinds of marriages. The first is the union of soul mates. These kindred souls are mates in the sense of being partners for the journey, coworkers and friends on the path of life.

Soul mates are learning the same lessons dealing with a similar karma and often work together for a common mission. If soul mates have completed constructive labors together in past lives, they may be assigned an even greater responsibility and mission together in this life. In a sense, soul mates are playmates in the schoolroom of life. You may have a number of such associations in the history of your soul's incarnations.

The second kind of relationship is the union of twin flames. Your twin flame is your other half, your counterpart. Created together in the beginning, you and your twin flame are the only two souls who share your unique pattern of identity. You may or may not be happily united with your twin flame in this life. Your twin flame may not even be in embodiment at this time. Whatever the situation, at inner levels your souls are one in the wholeness of your divine reality.

We incarnated with our twin flame—one of us the masculine and the other the feminine polarity of the Divine Whole—to fulfill a mission together and to grow spiritually. We would have continued to share the beauty of our relationship as cosmic lovers through our many incarnations on earth if we had remained in harmony with our original nature, with each other and with God. When we fell from that state of perfection, we created negative karma with each other and with others. Our entanglements with others demanded that we reembody with them in order to resolve the karma we had created. As one karmic circumstance led to another, we found ourselves farther and farther apart from our first love.

Plato spoke of the innate desire of twin flames to find one another. Man, he wrote in his *Symposium,* "is always looking for his other half." He said, "Ancient is the desire of one another which is implanted in us, reuniting our original nature, making one of two, and healing the state of man." When twin souls meet, says Plato, "the pair are lost in an amazement of love and friendship and intimacy."

Sometimes because we haven't used the opportunity life has given us to the fullest, we are like ships passing in the night, not knowing how near and yet how far we are from our twin flame. I remember one such embodiment when I was born into a poor family in Paris. I spent my life raising my many children, doing the wash and gossiping over the back fence. As far as my soul's estimate is concerned, it was a very uneventful and unfruitful life.

We've all had great embodiments and we've all had embodiments where we made more karma than we balanced. It's the nature of human experience. Karma takes us where we have to go, not necessarily where we want to go, but it's up to us to make the best use of that journey for our soul's growth.

When I was on my deathbed at the end of that life in Paris, my family called in the nearest priest to perform the last rites. It just so happened that a priest who was traveling around France was in the neighborhood. He came in, said the prayers and performed the blessing. He was just a humble priest passing by, but certainly not by chance.

As he leaned over me, he looked into my eyes and I recognized his eyes. They were the eyes of my twin flame, whom I recognized in this life as Mark Prophet. One look into those eyes and I saw the vision of our destiny. Through this devout soul, this dedicated priest, I realized I had wasted my life. So as I took my last breath, I cried out *"une autre opportunité"*—another opportunity. That was one of those brief encounters you can have with your twin flame that ties you together once more and prepares you to meet again in the future.

Sometimes our karma and our love take us around the world and back again. From the time Adrian was a small boy, he was fixated on Russia. When he was five, he worked out a scheme to earn money so he could go to Russia and free the people from Communism. He loved learning about that country and would often include the Russian people in his prayers at night. At thirteen, he wanted to move to Russia.

After graduating from high school, Adrian enrolled in a summer college course to study in Russia for six weeks. He had taken only half a semester of Russian. After he arrived there, he purposely didn't spend time with his fellow American students and would only communicate with Russians. In just two months, he was speaking the language. Three months later he was so fluent that the Russians he met thought he was from the Baltic States since he had only a slight accent.

For some time his new girlfriend, Alexia, didn't even know he was American. She attended college with him and thought he was a poor Russian student. After a year, they moved to America and have been together ever since. What drove Adrian half way around the world? Perhaps his past lives or some leftover karma he had yet to resolve there. Maybe it was his twin flame tugging on his soul. As Alexia's mother says, "Adrian came over here to find Alexia."

Sometimes the drama doesn't unfold so neatly. Even if we find our twin flame, we may encounter obstacles to our union until we tend to first things first. We may have to take care of unfinished business—first resolving karma we have made with others—before we can be with our twin flame again.

The Zohar, the major work of Kabbalah, says that God will bring us together with our twin flame when we live a life of purity and good works—in other words, when we balance the karma that separates us. "Happy the man who is upright in his works and walks in the way of truth," the Zohar tells us, "so that his soul may find its original mate, for then he becomes indeed perfect."

What we also learn along life's way is that finding our twin flame does not magically transport us into a perfect relationship—because we have plenty of unresolved karma with our twin flame too! A relationship between twin flames can be as difficult, if not more so, than any other marriage or partnership because in the past they have probably betrayed and hurt one another.

As you work on your own spiritual path, expanding the capacity of your heart to give and receive more love, you will magnetize your twin flame at the right time and the right place, whether in this life or beyond. Yet that's not our soul's primary goal. Karma and reincarnation teach us that our aim is not so much to find our first love as it is just to love.

No matter what kind of close relationship we have, all love is really love for our twin flame and love for God. All love moves us closer to reunion with our twin flame and with God. Love and only love will bring us back together. Love and only love will balance the karma that keeps us from inner wholeness as well as divine wholeness with our twin flame. Rather than turning our gaze here and there in search of "the one," we can begin walking the road to our greatest love starting right where we are.

❦   •

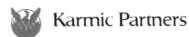

Karmic Partners

*Marriage is the opportunity for two
imperfect individuals to help each other
discharge their respective karmic debts,
forge new qualities of soul, and advance
in spiritual understanding and strength.*
— DR. GINA CERMINARA

In addition to the union of twin flames and soul
mates, there are also those close encounters of
the third kind—karmic marriages. Sometimes we
see two people who seem to have little in common.
What they do have in common is karma.

In a karmic marriage, individuals are drawn
together to balance mutual karma with each other.
They may also have mutual karma with other
souls. Before coming into embodiment, a husband
and wife may have agreed to bring into the world
certain children who are a part of their group
karma.

Your soul knows why you are in a karmic
relationship. You may have been told by your spiritual teachers or guardian angel: You and this person abused each other in a past life. Or by your

neglect, by your failure to act, you once caused the ruin of this town. Or because you walked away from your responsibility, many people died in a famine. Now you must serve together to set things right.

These are not unlikely situations. The ramifications of what we do by our selfishness or by refusing to serve life are great. At inner levels the soul who is on the path back to God desires to do whatever she must do in order to right the wrongs of the past. She knows that this is the only way to get back to the spiritual bliss she started from.

Karmic marriages are sometimes marked by a love-hate relationship. The partners never seem to stop fighting and yet they are miserable without each other. They seem to love intensely and to hate intensely.

This is one of those paradoxes of life that only makes sense in the context of karma and reincarnation. Often the most magnetic attractions are based on a past-life liaison of intense hatred, hurt or even violence. Frequently, the only way we can overcome the karma stemming from a severe crime or betrayal is by expressing intense love in a husband-wife relationship. The universal law of karma necessitates that whenever we have hated another, we must give love to balance that karma and quell the raging fires of hate.

Karmic relationships can be difficult as old wounds are reopened and karmic encounters are revisited. Yet they are important precisely because they give us the opportunity to apply the unguent of love to heal those wounds. They also help us master negative patterns that are keeping us from opening our heart to give and receive more love.

While any marriage can have its challenges, it can have its rewards as well, for we also bring to our relationships the fruit of our good karma together. We can share our gifts of love and mutual support even while we are working out the kinks of our karma.

In this day and age, we are winding up the loose ends of our karma with a number of people, and therefore we may experience in this lifetime several kinds of relationships—those of soul mates, twin flames and karmic partners. Whatever the relationship, it's not karma or lack of it that is the decisive factor in its success. It's what we do to love our way through our challenges and our karma that can make or break a relationship.

A Prisoner of Love

What determines how much karma you balance in this life?... It is how much love you inject into what you are doing.

—SAINT GERMAIN

Sometimes the force of attraction between two people is irresistible. At first, there is no one in the world we would rather be with. The love is there, the thrill of the new relationship is there, and sooner or later we may even decide to marry. We all know the expression "the honeymoon is over." That means our karma has hit. Now the work of the heart must begin.

But why were we so attracted to each other in the first place? Although we may have much karma to balance with our husband or wife, the initial impact was exhilarating because at the subconscious level we were elated that we had found the person with whom we could balance that karma.

When the honeymoon is over, what keeps us going and giving is our soul knowing that we must get through our karmic obligations before we can move on to the next spiral of life and the projects closest to our heart. We sense that the faster we submit to the law of our karma—which is the law of love—the faster we and our partner will both be liberated from that karma.

Sometimes when the karma is resolved, the relationship actually dissolves. There is nothing remaining to hold it together, and people move on because they are called to work on new assignments.

I have found that God often gives us the gift of intense love in the face of intense karma for the healing of the old wounds. The capacity to love and the release of love is something that seems to happen without our consciously willing it. We feel like the prisoner of this love. Our rational mind may be telling us we should not be loving this person, but the heart loves on.

I have studied this phenomenon in myself, because we really have nowhere else to go but to the laboratory of our own being to learn the lessons of life. Without my will at all, my heart would become on fire with love for certain people. I did not create this love. I didn't start the fire. God put it in my heart.

If I roll back the years and think about my

high school days, I can recognize when God had placed that kind of love in my heart for someone. Just seeing that person would create within me a heart full of love. Again, I never started the love. The love was there and I observed it, and then I was its prisoner. In cases like these our karma, seeking resolution, brings us together, and our Higher Self sheds immense love and forgiveness to help us resolve that karma.

It's as if we are drenching the other person in love. When enough love has flowed to balance the karma, all of a sudden the faucet turns off and we no longer have this intense and compelling feeling of love. It's almost unbelievable in contrast to the way we felt before. I've seen this in my own life. I poured out the love, the karma was balanced, and I walked on.

I had this experience after I met my first husband. I was working in a Christian Science church and I saw this young man, about five years older than I. He was a leader in the youth fellowship and a law student. The first time I saw him a block away, I recognized him and he recognized me. When I met him, an inner voice said to me, "You must serve him." "How?" I asked. "You can help him in his work. You can help him with the youth group."

So this is what I did. When he became sick, I again heard that voice. "Go and take care of him," it said. I kept on receiving these inner instructions and I kept obeying them. Then one day, he asked me to marry him. We had a small wedding in New Jersey. As I walked down the aisle, I heard the voice within me again. "It is but for a little while." I was stunned. I had believed that marriage was for keeps.

We had both been going to school in Boston, but in order to support him through college I set aside my own education for a time. I worked, kept house and cooked his meals. About ten months later, I found the spiritual path I had been looking for all my life and I told him about it. He said that I would have to choose between him and that path. I had to let him go because I knew in my heart that I had found my reason for being.

Later I came to understand that if I had not made the sacrifices I did for him, I would not have been able to move on in my career or meet and marry Mark Prophet, my twin flame. I learned from this not to be afraid to obey the voice within, to serve others or to sacrifice on anyone's behalf.

You never know when the gift you are giving is paying the last farthing of some karma that will liberate you to move on to a higher calling.

We may never know exactly what the past-life episode was that created our karmic debt, but we can usually figure out what we must do now to balance it. Ask yourself: What quality or virtue am I being asked to master? Maybe you mistreated your partner (or child or coworker) in some way in the past and now you must show them a tender and loving regard. Perhaps you ignored your partner's needs, prevented him from going forward with his career or somehow cut short his life, and now you must sacrifice for a time so he can have a second chance.

I believe it's important to work, and work hard, at a marriage. We are in our relationships for a reason. It's tempting to walk away from unpleasant situations, to treat them half-heartedly, or to just bide our time until "the real thing comes along." That's a good way to prolong the resolution of karma—and to make more of it.

If we walk out on our spiritual duty, we will only have to face the same individuals and the same karmic elements again. Our future relationships, one after the other, will most likely bring us nose to nose with the same kind of issues and the same kind of anguish we saw the first time.

When a situation is staring you in the face, look at it as an optimal opportunity, for you never know how long you will have to wait for that opportunity to come around again. You can choose to melt down the hardness of heart and the karma with the fervent heat of love, or you can choose to part with animosity, which only delays the day of reckoning. That doesn't mean you have to remain in a karmic relationship forever. But you may have to work hard to find the reason for the relationship and then make certain that you balance the karma so that both of you leave the relationship with a feeling of resolution.

Where do we start? We start with ourselves. We can't really change how another person will act; we can only change how we will react. We can determine that we will stick with a situation until we have conquered our jealousy, our resentment, our pride or our anger. We can stick with it until we have brought our partner everything we can and until we can say, "I feel nothing toward this individual but love, and I am loving no matter what he or she says or does."

Of course, both partners have to be willing to work in harmony. If only one person makes the effort, it can be difficult. If it becomes impossible to resolve karma at a personal level because the relationship is breeding more harm than good and we are only re-creating old patterns, we may have to end the relationship and turn to other ways of balancing the karma.

In addition, it's important to realize that there may come a time in a karmic relationship when our mutual obligation is over. Out of habit, we can say to ourselves, "I'm supposed to be loving this person. I'm supposed to keep this relationship going." There's a certain security in the familiar, and we can become complacent in a situation rather than move on when it's time.

How will you know when you have settled the old accounts? When they are settled, you will sense a resolution and an inner peace. There will no longer be the same intensity binding you together. In situations like these, we have to go into our heart and, through deep prayer, meditation and soul searching, attune with God to get the right answers.

Not All Relationships Are Healthy

The difficulty in life is the choice.
—GEORGE MOORE

You will meet key people in your life that you feel you have known before. You sense that you have work to do with them, whether through a business, a creative partnership or a marriage. There will be other encounters where you feel an immediate attraction or recognition, but you also sense danger or feel unexplainably ill at ease.

Pay attention to those feelings. Just because you have known someone or have even been married to them in a previous life, it does not mean you have to get involved with them in this life. Someday you may bump into a person with whom you have intense karma or deep emotional ties, but together you will end up reenacting old, dysfunctional patterns instead of transcending them. This kind of relationship can pull you down and through it you can make karma instead of balancing it.

You may have only a few months' worth of karma to work out with this person. You can render whatever service you feel compelled to give him or her along life's way, but you do not have to become entangled in a relationship that is abusive or detrimental to your spiritual growth. Relationships are not meant to drag us down.

So in the realm of relationships, we don't want to skip an opportunity to give some gift from our heart to resolve karma when that is what we are called to do. At the same time, we don't want to get entrenched in a situation that causes us to create more karma and ultimately take a wrong turn on our spiritual path.

You always have a choice. You can decide if you are or if you are not going to get involved with someone you are attracted to. When making a decision to get married, for instance, you can ask yourself, "Do I want to share this person's karma?" For when we vow to support another "for richer, for poorer, in sickness and in health," that means "in cycles of karma—the good and the not so good."

When you marry, you take on your partner's karma in the sense that you have vowed to support him through thick and thin. This is how it should be. We love so much that we want with all of our heart to support each other in every way we can. Marriage with the right person can be a beautiful and fulfilling journey.

Before we can fully take advantage of the wonderful opportunities for transformation that karma does offer us, we have to learn to discern the myths that have crept into the Western understanding of karma and reincarnation. In part 3, we'll expose some of these common karmic traps.

PART 3

Karmic Traps

*To see what is in front of one's nose
needs a constant struggle.*

—GEORGE ORWELL

The Cup of Forgetfulness

There have been thousands of changes in form. Look always to the form in the present; for, if you think of the forms in the past, you will separate yourself from your true Self.

—RUMI

If we have lived before, why don't we remember who we were? And do we have to know about our past lives to resolve the karma from those lives?

Greek mythology tells us that souls who have just passed on and those ready to reincarnate have to drink from the river Lethe, whose waters make the soul forget her previous life. The Gnostic text *Pistis Sophia* speaks of the soul drinking "the water of forgetfulness." Dr. Ian Stevenson reported that many of those in Thailand who had past-life memories claimed to remember being offered the "fruit of forgetfulness" before being reborn.

The veil of forgetfulness descends for a reason. That reason is mercy. As Gandhi once said, "It is nature's kindness that we do not remember past births.... Life would be a burden if we carried such a tremendous load of memories." That's exactly what happened to both Shanti Devi and Peter, whose stories we told earlier. After Shanti met her parents from her previous life, she burst into tears and had to be forcibly separated from them to return to her present-day family.

The young boy Peter, as you will recall, was obsessed with his former life as a policeman. In his case, since his parents didn't understand what was happening and didn't know how to handle it—his mother actually told him to stop making up stories —he didn't have the support or the tools he needed to deal with it.

"It certainly didn't help Peter [to recall his past life], and seemed to make his adjustment to this life more difficult," wrote Dr. Helen Wambach. She concluded that "a premature immersion in experiences that may have been traumatic merely adds to the burden of adjustment in our present life."[1] With the proper teaching and care, however, children who do have past-life memories can be helped to understand and work through them.

Dr. Christopher Bache points out another reason for sealing the memories of the past. "In isolating us from our larger identity," he says, "our amnesia intensifies our learning experience by focusing us completely on the experience in which we are presently engaged. When we are distracted and give only half our attention to what we are working on, the results usually show it."[2] Dr. Joel Whitton and Joe Fisher add that "just as it is pointless for a student to be furnished with answers before sitting down to write an examination, so the test of life requires that certain information is temporarily withheld from the conscious mind."[3]

A past-life memory is not something to be taken lightly. When you become aware of a past life, the karma of that embodiment comes to the fore. You can no longer ignore it. You may even become burdened by the memories. So one reason the records of past lives should not be opened prematurely is that we're not always ready to deal with them or with the karma they bring into our lives. That's why God only lifts the veil on our past lives when there is something our soul must learn from that memory and we can handle it.

I have had people tell me that a fortune-teller revealed a past life to them when they were a teenager, and they still can't get it out of their head a decade or two later. They became preoccupied with that one piece of information rather than keeping their attention and their energy focused on moving forward and balancing their karma in the present, which is where we must deal with it. In some cases, they became overwhelmed by self-condemnation and guilt.

An additional word of caution: Just because someone is psychic or claims to be, it does not mean that everything that comes through him or her is 100 percent accurate or that it's the full picture. Also, it's important to keep in mind that the place where our past-life records are sealed is a very private place within us and one that we may not want to readily invite others into.

Every one of us has had constructive lives as well as lives that were not so constructive. We do not, however, have to know all the details to transmute the negative karma and make spiritual progress. The conditions right in front of us are a road map to our assignments for this lifetime.

 # Karma Isn't Fate

Karma is of great importance,
but of greater gravity is the choice.
Karma is but the condition of the choice.

—EL MORYA

Whatever you are or are not, you earned it— the good, the bad and the irksome. This is the nature of karma.

Whatever you are or are not, you can change it. This too is the nature of karma. That's because *karma isn't fate.*

Karma can help us understand how we got where we are—the circumstances of our life, the events that take shape around us, the people we seem to magnetize. But it doesn't tell us how we will respond to those circumstances, events and people. That's entirely up to us, and that's what determines our destiny. We exercised free will to create karma. We can exercise free will to transform it. The only boundaries to our progress are the ones we ourselves have put in place.

If our karma dictates an untimely death, it is possible, for example, to earn a life extension by a change of heart. When we serve life with all of our heart, life will give back to us. Nothing is final until we make it final and nothing is predestined until we make it our destiny.

Dr. Whitton's research into what takes place between lives also reveals that there are karmic "tests" built into our life plan. Whether or not we pass these tests determines how fast we will progress in this life. He gives the dramatic example of a young man, Steve, who disliked his father.

When his father lay ill in a Miami nursing home, Steve rarely went to see the old man. One day he had an impulse to visit his dad. While there, he noticed that his father's respirator tube had become dislodged and he was therefore having a hard time breathing. Steve had a choice—he could either let his father die or run for the nurse. He thought it over for a moment and then shouted for the nurse, who replaced the tube.

Later, at age twenty-nine, Steve was hit broadside by a truck while riding his bicycle. The accident could have been fatal, but he was fortunate to have escaped with only a fractured femur. In his early forties, Steve learned under hypnosis that there was a strong connection between these two events and that he had known about it before he was born. "My karmic script clearly stated that the life-or-death incident with my father was most definitely a very important test that I had set myself," he said. "If I could forgive him his transgressions against me— which appeared to extend over several lifetimes— I would not be killed in the bicycle accident."

What is even more interesting is that Steve said that based on his past behavior, it was expected that he would probably allow his dad to die. Since he passed his test instead, his first life plan had come to an end and "sketchy plans for future lives had been brought forward to operate in the current life."[4] His choices determined his fate, not the other way around.

 ## Going Nowhere Fast

The best way out is always through.

—ROBERT FROST

Another karmic trap is the temptation to avoid our karma. Lifetime after lifetime we may bump into a certain challenge, but because we don't realize that it is an opportunity in disguise, we run in the opposite direction to avoid the karmic encounter. Or we react the way we did when we first made the karma—with anger or impatience or criticism—which only gets us more entangled.

When we start seeing things from the perspective of karma, we realize that unless we embrace the karmic tests staring us in the face, we will have to keep reincarnating with the same individuals or in the same kinds of circumstances until we determine to pass those tests. Turning our back only postpones the day when we must stand, face and conquer.

It's natural to want to avoid the friction of karmic encounters. Those clashes often make us look at a part of ourselves we would rather not look at. Yet God deliberately brings together individuals whose karmic patterns grate on each other so that they can knock the rough edges off of one another, so to speak. As the master El Morya has taught, "There is a certain friction that is required for all attainment on the path." If someone in your life brings out the worst in you, praise God. You might never have seen that sharp edge otherwise; and until you make it smooth, everyone who bumps into you will feel that sharpness.

Recognizing when we're going nowhere fast because we are trying to avoid our karma can be subtle, especially in a culture that tends to breed the desire for quick fixes to life's inconveniences and pain. Yet pain is an incredible teacher. It signals us that something in our life is out of kilter, out of alignment with our inner blueprint. Whether it's soul pain or physical pain, all pain is a growing pain.

Someone may come along and rearrange the molecules of your life and you may suddenly have comfort instead of pain, wealth instead of poverty. But you may not have begun to deal with the deep things you came into embodiment to resolve.

We may find it easy to take a job like our neighbor's and have a comfortable lifestyle like our neighbor's because it insulates us from our karma or our duty to life. That cushion, however, may be compromising our spiritual path if our karma and our duty is calling us elsewhere. Maybe our parents expected us to be a lawyer or a doctor, but our heart tells us we need to be a social worker or an inner-city teacher.

Perhaps the most extreme form of avoidance is suicide. Yet suicide is never an escape. Leo Tolstoy once wrote in his diary, "How interesting it would be to write the story of the experiences in this life of a man who killed himself in his previous life; how he now stumbles against the very demands which had offered themselves before, until he arrives at the realization that he must fulfill those demands."

Tolstoy was right. Those who commit suicide will have to face the same karmic dramas once again—and quickly—for they will be immediately sent back into embodiment to pick up where they left off. They will be born into a situation where they will have to deal with the same karmic issues all over again.

Those who suffer and are suicidal need our prayers and support. What greater lifeboat can we offer than the story of their soul's journey, their true reason for being and the beautiful possibilities that are open to them? Every one of us needs to feel valued for the spiritual being that we are and encouraged to press forward on our individual path of spiritual growth.

The Sense of Injustice

*The tragedy of life is not so much what
men suffer, but rather what they miss.*

—THOMAS CARLYLE

One of the biggest karma-making traps is to allow ourselves to get entangled with someone in an emotional ping-pong match. When you hear that defensive voice inside your head saying, "He hurt me, he has it in for me, he can't push me around like that—I'm going to get back at him," watch out. You're headed into the web. It's the web of action-reaction.

The tempter says, "Go ahead, get angry, lash out—*come down to my level.*" As soon as we start rolling in the mud and fighting it out at the lowest common denominator of action-reaction, it's hard to extricate ourselves from the web. Tempers flare and before we know it we have made more karma than we started with. If we don't stop the vicious circle and take the high road, we will have to keep coming back to clean up our mess—today, tomorrow or even in another lifetime. That high road starts with forgiveness.

Yet it's hard to forgive in the face of tragedy. When tragedy strikes, the temptation is to blame ourselves or even to become angry at God. The anger, however, won't erase the pain or help nurture our soul through the ordeal. It will only make matters worse. In most cases, we can never know for sure the inner dynamics that ignited the tragedy, but we can choose to open our heart and discover the profound message that is meant for us.

I know a mother, Marie, who found out after she had been pregnant for almost nine months that her baby had a fatal chromosome problem. This meant that the child would die within a few minutes of birth—if she survived the stress of labor.

When Marie called to tell me this, I comforted her and explained that God doesn't do anything without a profound purpose, and he had drawn her family into that purpose for a deep reason. I said that souls come into embodiment to learn lessons and to give us lessons. I also told Marie that by carrying this child, she had helped that soul balance a tremendous karma.

When the baby was born, all of three pounds, she surpassed everyone's expectations. She survived labor and with oxygen she stayed alive for seventy days. Her parents named her Catherine. This little one was incredibly courageous. Not only did she volunteer to be born with this chromosome condition and therefore serious internal defects, but she chose to stay in that body for ten weeks so she could balance even more karma.

Although the experience of losing Catherine was extremely painful, knowing about karma and reincarnation helped Marie tremendously. She still had to work through her pain and learn to surren der to God's plan, but she didn't have those gnawing questions *why me? why her?* She didn't blame herself and she didn't blame God. In fact, Marie says that the pain of the experience brought her a kind of resolution. She feels she had lost children in other lives and denied the pain.

I had the sense that Marie, her husband and their four-year-old daughter would see Catherine again on the highway of life and I told them that. Marie later said to me, "The entire time Catherine was alive, I just looked into her eyes and asked God to please help me recognize her when I saw her again."

A year and a half after Catherine's passing, Marie became pregnant and she gave birth to a healthy seven pound, six ounce baby girl, Crystal. Was it the soul of Catherine come again? "I definitely related to her as Catherine when she was born," says Marie. "Crystal had this little cry that sounded just like Catherine." A couple of months before Crystal turned two, she suddenly told her sitter: "I had tiny fingers and then I died." Recently the family was looking at pictures of Catherine. A few hours later, Crystal looked up and said, "When my name was Catherine, Diedre held me." (Diedre is her older sister.)

In Catherine's case, I believe that her parents had volunteered to be there for her while she was expiating her karma in that little body. Sometimes that's why we're part of a tragic scene. We volunteered to help out. But Marie feels that she also learned much from Catherine.

"I believe Catherine came to teach us about love, determination and courage," she says. "From Catherine I learned compassion for all life and especially for people with birth defects. She helped me learn to trust God more, to love more selflessly and to be more compassionate. She taught me to let go. And she showed me that you can be instrumental in helping someone else balance their karma." We make spiritual progress when, like Marie, we not only play our part with courage but also listen for the lesson.

Not Everything Is
the Result of Karma

*If you judge people, you have
no time to love them.*

—MOTHER TERESA

Life is intricate. Not everything can be categorized into neat generalities, even in our spiritual life. Yes, the circumstances of life are the result of our good and not-so-good thoughts, words and deeds come full circle. But not always.

I once participated in a theological dialogue that was part of a seminar on "The Gospel and the New Age." One minister asked, "If we should find ourselves experiencing what seems to be great and disproportionate suffering, should we conclude that it's something we deserve because we have set in motion forces of cause and effect either in this life or in a previous life?"

I told him that we can't conclude that everything that happens to us is karma. Jesus, for example, told his followers that they would be persecuted as he was. And it's important to remember that people do initiate new acts of negative karma every day and innocent souls can fall prey to their schemes.

In addition, whatever our chosen spiritual path, we will meet challenges that are for the testing of our mettle, as in the case of Job, whom God allowed to be tested by Satan. God may test us over and over to see if we have mastered a particular virtue. If we tend to be stingy, for example, God may put us in situations that give us the opportunity to open our heart and give more of ourselves.

The minister also asked me, "Whether it's karma or persecution, should our response still be the same?" I said that, whatever the case, if we have so-called enemies, we must bless them, send them love and light, and pray for them. Our response has to be positive, fair and loving. Ask yourself, "What would Jesus do?"—or what would Buddha or Krishna or Abraham or Mary or Saint Teresa or any of the great adepts and saints do?

Another reason we may feel burdened or

things don't seem to be going right is that there are forces of the human ego that oppose the good we would do and the good we are to reap. As the saying goes, "No good deed goes unpunished." You may find, for example, that those who are jealous of your loving relationship or your new endeavor will try to destroy it. That is why an important part of the path of love is learning to guard the heart as well as to open it, a subject we talk about in our book *Alchemy of the Heart.*[3]

In other cases, we may experience a certain condition because God wants us to get in touch with the pain that others bear so we can rise to a new level of understanding and compassion. There is yet another reason souls may suffer or bear a burden—they volunteer to make sacrifices to help someone close to them learn an important soul lesson. At times the saints, through their intense physical suffering, were balancing world karma and not their own. They were shouldering the sins (i.e., karma) of the world to give others an expanded opportunity to grow.

In her book *Embraced by the Light,* Betty Eadie tells the poignant story of one man's sacrifice for his friend, a prominent attorney. During her near-death experience described in the book, Eadie was shown this man, a drunk, lying on the sidewalk in a large city. As she told her escorts, he's "a drunken bum lying in his wallow," and she didn't understand why she needed to see him. Her escorts then revealed the inner story.

"His spirit was revealed to me, and I saw a magnificent man, full of light," she says. "Love emanated from his being, and I understood that he was greatly admired in the heavens. This great being came to earth as a teacher to help a friend that he had spiritually bonded with."[6]

He had volunteered to play the role of drunk for his friend, the attorney. Passing by the drunk on his way to the office, the attorney, a naturally compassionate man, would be stirred to greater generosity and to share his abundance with others. Eadie understood that although neither would remember their inner pact, they would nevertheless fulfill their missions. Her lesson, she says, was about accepting all people and not judging from outer appearances.

Souls do volunteer to sacrifice on behalf of loved ones, and therefore we can never criticize or judge another who is going through difficult times.

We never know whether someone is an innocent victim, the victimizer from a previous life who is receiving back his karma, or a soul who is making a sacrifice on someone's behalf, perhaps even our own.

Jesus said the same thing when he challenged the popular view of his day that suffering was always a punishment for sin. Some Galileans had been murdered while offering their sacrifices. When Jesus heard about it, he asked, "Do you think that these Galileans were worse sinners than all the other Galileans, because they suffered thus? I tell you, No; but unless you repent you will all likewise perish."

In other words, we can never point an accusing finger. We can never say that someone who is healthy is a saint or that someone who is sick is a sinner. We can never assume that someone who is rich has good karma or that another person who is poor has bad karma. Again, our perspective is not always the soul's perspective.

 The Soul's Ascent

When you make the two one, and when
you make the inside like the outside and the
outside like the inside, and the above like the
below,... then you will enter [the kingdom].

THE GOSPEL OF THOMAS

Another trap, and the last one we'll deal with here, is the false belief that there will be no end to the rounds of rebirth. Hindu and Buddhist traditions tell us that our karma requires us to keep reincarnating—but only until we have balanced our karmic debts and achieved reunion with the Divine.

The truth is that reincarnation has a purpose. That purpose is the soul's ascent. We're not supposed to keep going around in circles, rebirth after rebirth ad infinitum. We're supposed to be ascending a spiral higher and higher, becoming more and more of our Higher Self. When we are no longer weighted down by our negative karma and we have become one with our Higher Self, our soul can rise at last to her true spiritual stature and be free of the wheel of rebirth.

Our lifetimes are only stepping-stones to that ultimate goal of oneness with our spiritual self and with the Universal Spirit. As the famous Hermetic axiom puts it, As above so below. We are meant to become below (on earth, in matter) the mirror image of that which is above (our Higher Self, one with Spirit). When the image below matches the image above, time and space collapse and the soul ascends to its point of origin in Spirit. The soul still retains, however, her unique identity the unique way she expresses her spirituality and has integrated with her spiritual self. No two souls do it the same way, and that is what is so wonderful about this universe.

One way to think about our goal in life is that our entire reason for being born into these physical bodies is to access the light of the Spirit, to draw it down into every cell and atom of these minds, emotions and bodies that we wear until they become that light. When that takes place—when what is below is as above—there is no longer any difference between us and our divine reality.

The reason we have embodied again and again is that we haven't contained enough light. We have been weighted down by the unfinished business of our karma and by our desires for the things of this world. When we let go of our karmic baggage and embody the light of the Spirit, we ascend in consciousness. We become masters of our destiny and qualify to graduate from earth's schoolroom.

When we have mastered the requirements of our karma and fulfilled our unique divine plan— our dharma, or duty to life—our soul can reunite with Spirit in the ritual of the ascension. At that moment we will become *ascended* masters, just like the adepts and saints of East and West who have also fulfilled their reason for being.

In past ages, individuals were required to balance 100 percent of their karma before they could be free of the rounds of rebirth. As mankind prepared to enter the new two-thousand-year period called the Aquarian age, we were given a dispensation—we could choose to ascend with only 51 percent of our karma balanced. We could then work from inner planes with those still incarnated on earth to balance the remaining 49 percent of our karmic debts.

In other words, just over half of all the energies we've ever misused in all of our embodiments must be brought back into harmony with our original nature. At that point, we can decide if we want to come back in a physical body to continue to serve humanity or if we want to become an ascended master. In Buddhism those who elect, out of supreme love, to remain on earth are called bodhisattvas.

One of the reasons that the requirement was changed is that after we have balanced 51 percent, we meet some of the most challenging aspects of our karma. Therefore, if we are not careful, we could actually make more karma after that point and fall back into deeper levels of karma. It's much easier to descend the mountain than it is to climb up.

Neither this life nor your ascension will be the end of your spiritual journey. The sacred adventure will live on. Whether we are in physical embodiment or not, our soul always has the grand opportunity to explore new levels of the inner world and expand her spiritual mastery. When you are finally on your way Home, you will transcend this narrow spectrum of experience called earth and move on to higher dimensions of reality.

In our final section, part 4, we'll talk about some of the practical steps we can take to transcend our karmic past, transform our future and fulfill our soul's destiny.

The Chart of Your Divine Self illustrates the soul's potential and the ultimate goal of our incarnation on earth. This chart is a diagram of your spiritual anatomy and your potential to become who you really are.

The upper figure is the I AM Presence, the Presence of God that is individualized in each one of us. Buddhists call it the *Dharmakaya,* the body of Ultimate Reality. Your I AM Presence is your personalized "I AM THAT I AM," the name of God that was revealed to Moses. "I AM THAT I AM" means simply but profoundly *As above, so below. As God is in heaven, so God is on earth within me.*

Your I AM Presence is surrounded by seven concentric spheres of spiritual energy that make up what is called the causal body. These spheres of pulsating energy contain the record of the good works you have performed—your good karma.

The middle figure represents your Higher Self—your inner teacher, dearest friend and voice of conscience. Each of us is destined to embody the attributes of our Higher Self, which is sometimes referred to as the inner Buddha or the inner Christ, or Holy Christ Self.

The shaft of white light descending from the heart of the I AM Presence through the Higher Self to the lower figure is the crystal cord (or "silver cord," as Ecclesiastes calls it). It is the umbilical cord, or lifeline, that ties you to Spirit. Your

THE CHART OF YOUR DIVINE SELF

crystal cord also nourishes the divine spark that is ensconced in the secret chamber of your heart.

The lower figure represents you on the spiritual path, surrounded by the protective white light of God and the purifying spiritual fire of the Holy Spirit, known as the violet flame (see pages 194 and following). The purpose of your soul's evolution on earth is to grow in self-mastery, balance your karma, become one with your Higher Self and fulfill your unique mission so that you can return to the spiritual dimensions that are your real home.

When "the below" (your soul in embodiment, the lower figure) becomes as "the above" (your Higher Self, the middle figure), your soul then reunites with your I AM Presence (the upper figure), free at last of the rounds of rebirth. The three figures in the Chart of Your Divine Self become one.

PART 4

Karmic Transformations

Why stay we on the earth
except to grow?

—ROBERT BROWNING

Taking the Higher Perspective

There is no object on earth which cannot
be looked at from a cosmic point of view.
—FYODOR DOSTOYEVSKY

Transformation begins with a change in perspective, a paradigm shift. It required us to go deep within to gain a heart perspective. It also requires us to climb to a higher vantage where the details become less sharp but the setting and the context more clear. That context almost always involves karma and reincarnation.

Once I was with a group of people in San Francisco, one of whom was an older gentleman. As we all got out of the car, I accidentally slammed the door on his hand. Although it wasn't a serious injury, it was painful. You can imagine how profoundly sorry and apologetic I was. I couldn't believe I had done such a thing.

Then he said something I will never forget. He looked at me and said, "That's all right. I did this to another person one day, and so now you have allowed me to balance my karma." Whether or not this man was correct, I thought about that remark and about his attitude for a long time. How quick he was to take that higher perspective.

The same lesson comes to us in the old Tibetan tale about a venerable Buddhist monk who was mistakenly accused of stealing and killing a cow, even though he was a vegetarian. The monk was chained and put into a hole in the ground, yet he did not say a word to defend himself. Although the cow was found a few days later, the man responsible for the monk's release got caught up in timely matters and forgot about the prisoner. The monk remained in the pit for months.

At last, one of his disciples obtained an audience with the king and told him what had happened. The king rushed to set the monk free and begged the old man's forgiveness, promising to punish those who were responsible. The monk, however, implored the king to punish no one.

"It was my turn to suffer," he admitted, explaining that in a past life he had stolen a baby cow. While escaping from his pursuers, he had abandoned it near a holy man meditating in the forest. The holy man was blamed for the crime and chained in a hole for six days. "I have been waiting lifetimes to expiate my sin," said the old man, "and I am grateful to your subjects for bringing me the opportunity to be free of this karma."

Spiritually as well as physically, energy can neither be created nor destroyed, as the Law of the Conservation of Energy tells us. Three embodiments ago our intense rage may have set off a chain reaction that caused harm to others. We've forgotten all about that rampage, but that energy is still in circulation, stamped with negativity.

Now we have a problem in our life and we say, "How can God allow this? If there is a God in the universe, why did he allow me to get into this terrible accident? Why am I constantly surrounded by verbally abusive people? Why did my child die stillborn?" We become angry with God because we don't realize that *we* are God—we are the God of our own universe. We have set in motion causes whose effects will return to us as surely as the sun rises every day.

Carrie learned this lesson over the course of a physically and emotionally painful experience. Several years ago she was in a boating accident with her boyfriend, David. Caught in the wake of a larger boat, their small speedboat was rocked by the waves. Each time the waves carried the little boat up with the crest of the wave and down again, her body slammed against the deck. She was in excruciating pain, and for the next three months she couldn't sit comfortably or go to work.

David had been driving the boat too fast and his recklessness had caused the accident, but he never took accountability for it. Meanwhile, Carrie's medical bill grew larger and larger and she depleted her savings trying to heal her back. David finally agreed to pay Carrie $500, which wasn't nearly enough to cover her bills. He gave her $250, but when they split up he never came through with the rest of the money.

At first Carrie was angry and upset about David's irresponsibility and her predicament, but then she began to look at things in a different light. "I started to focus on myself," she says. "I began to say to myself, 'What if you are getting back something that you gave to somebody else?' That was a moment of incredible enlightenment for me. I thought to myself, 'Whatever comes back on you, isn't it a better idea to respond with a higher intention and a higher action than to play victim?'"

Carrie also says she learned something she had never fully understood before—*that we have a choice*. "I learned that we can stay hurt and angry and have hateful feelings toward the other person," she explains, "or we can forgive them. We can stay in a dark place or go to a light place."

Carrie says that this accident, as painful as it was, became a positive force in her life. "This experience enabled me to forgive David and also to forgive myself—because I realized that I had probably been someone just like David and maybe worse. It's made me a more compassionate and tolerant person, and it has made me much more cognizant of my actions. Since then, when I'm faced with choices like these and I choose the higher path, I find that more doors open."

The story didn't end there. Like many of our painful experiences, something can trigger the emotions all over again. Years later, out of the blue, David e-mailed Carrie. He was now married and his wife was expecting a child. He had recently come across a book Carrie had given him years before and was reminded of the incident. David explained that he was really trying to live a more spiritual life, and he felt that he had not acted honorably in breaking his promise to Carrie. He offered to send her the remaining $250.

With that message, the memories and the hurt flooded into her world all over again. Most of her close friends told her not to give David the satisfaction of making good on his promise, and she tended to agree. One friend, though, took a different tack. He told her that David needed her acceptance for his own spiritual growth. Rebuffing him wasn't going to resolve anything. Bitterness would just prolong the karmic tie, but forgiveness would set them both free.

It was then that Carrie realized she was still playing a role in David's life, and he in hers. "In the larger scheme of things, it was no longer about the money but about his soul—and mine—needing completion," she says. "David was trying to make amends, and the least I could do was accept the gift." She told David to go ahead and send the check.

"Whether karma is coming back or whether it's one of those situations you create yourself because you very much want to learn the lesson, what matters is that you do learn the lesson and grow from it," Carrie now says. "We really need to look at the big picture and not be so self-motivated and selfish. For me, part of the lesson from this episode is to slow down and look at what you're doing. What you do *does* matter. It *does* have consequences for you, first and foremost, and for other people."

 Opening the Channels

To be wronged is nothing
unless you continue to remember it.
—CONFUCIUS

Forgiveness is always the beginning of the spiritual path, yet it is not necessarily easy, especially when grave crimes have been committed against body, mind or soul. What makes forgiveness even harder is that many of us have been erroneously taught that it wipes away the transgression or the crime. We think that when we ask for forgiveness or when we forgive another, that's the end of the matter. The perpetrator has no further responsibility.

This is a myth. Forgiveness does not equal absolution. We are still required to take full responsibility for our actions. If you steal something from someone, he may forgive you but you still need to return what you took or pay him back.

"Forgiveness of sins does not mean abrogation," Mark Prophet once taught. "God may overlook the fact that people made the error, and he may not demand immediate repayment—because if some people's debts were called in all at once, they would be spiritually bankrupt! So God says, 'Well, I'll forgive your sins.' But that doesn't mean that every wrong and every error we made is wiped out. We still have to balance the scales."

When God forgives us, our negative karma (or sin) is sealed for a time. It's as if God lifts a bundle of karma off our back so that it will be easier for us to walk the path of self-mastery and get ready to pass the exam when it comes around again.

That's how the universe works. If we lose our temper or get angry, we will be tested again on that formula of forgiveness and patience. The test may come in a new set of circumstances or it may appear as a replay of the same scenario with the same actors. Whatever the case, we will have to show how much love and forgiveness we can infuse into the situation to heal ourselves and to heal others.

Knowing how precisely the law of karma

operates frees us to surrender any situation into God's hands. We can forgive without condoning because we know that it is our job to dispense mercy and God's to dispense the justice that will help the soul learn her lessons. The when, where and how of that justice is God's business, not ours, which is what the Bible means when it says, "Vengeance is mine; I will repay, saith the Lord."

On a practical level, our lack of forgiveness can be de-energizing. Here is how it works: If we haven't "let go," the anger or resentment we hold on to keeps us tied to those we don't forgive. Our attention sets up a circuit of energy and, whether we are consciously aware of it or not, some of our energy is always flowing along that pathway, a prisoner of our mind and emotions. The energy that is trickling or rushing through that circuit, as the case may be, is not available for us to apply to our creative and loving endeavors.

"Attention is the key," says the master Saint Germain. "Where man's attention goes, there goes his energy." When we "forgive and forget," we release the energy we have invested in old patterns and put it back into circulation. Forgiveness, then, allows us to rechannel that energy into something more constructive. Just think of all the energy we can have when at the end of each day we let go of all sense of injustice, anger and even guilt about our own shortcomings.

Saint Germain also teaches that "if there is any part of life whom you have not forgiven for any wrong committed against you, real or imagined, you limit by that very resentment, by that very withholding of forgiveness, the amount of forgiveness you can receive for any and all karma." This is the same spiritual principle Jesus taught in the Lord's Prayer: "Forgive us our debts *as* we forgive our debtors." In other words, forgive us our own faults and mistakes *in the same manner as* we forgive the faults and mistakes of others. For we know that by the law of karma, only as we forgive another will we be forgiven.

Extending forgiveness as issues arise is one way to prevent karma from building up. It's the principle of "pay as you go." If there is someone you haven't forgiven or who hasn't forgiven you, talk to her or write a letter. Ask for her forgiveness and tell her that you forgive her. If the person has passed on, you can express your feelings in a written letter, burn it and ask the angels to deliver your letter to that soul.

You can also practice the art of forgiveness by creating your own surrender ritual, which you can give at the end of each day before going to sleep. If you are burdened by unresolved circumstances, you can ask God to forgive you, to help you forgive others and to reestablish a figure-eight flow of love between you and those you name. As part of that ritual, you can ask God to show you the practical steps to take the next day to move toward resolution. A universal prayer that has become a successful part of many people's surrender ritual is the affirmation for forgiveness, which is on page 209.

Sometimes God will unfold certain memories of past lives to show us how important it is to forgive. Donna, for instance, had a poignant past-life memory and meditation that showed her how energizing and healing forgiveness can be. In fact, it healed her of a chronic cough she had had for twelve years.

Donna had tried everything for her cough, but no medicine or treatment of any kind touched it. She began to think that it was rooted in some kind of past karma, although she had no idea what it was. Donna decided to try a meditation she had read about where you invite your inner teacher to help you contact and work through the record behind your illness. In her meditation, to her surprise, she met Jesus. "I will do anything you want me to do," she prayed to him. "I will go through anything you want me to go through. I will suffer anything you want me to suffer to get to this record."

Six days later Donna became very sick. The pain in her chest was excruciating. "It feels like a knife," she said to herself. "No, a tomahawk." It hurt so much that she could only breathe in tiny gasps. After three very long weeks, she was finally diagnosed with pneumonia and she began a course of medicine that led to her recovery.

Yet Donna couldn't shake the sense that the pain in her chest had felt like a tomahawk. She decided to go back into the meditation with her Higher Self to see if the tomahawk was part of the karmic record behind her chronic cough. That's when she saw the whole scenario.

"The first scene was of me lying in a covered wagon," she says. "I was expecting a baby. The covered wagons were gathered in a circle and the men were fighting the Indians. My husband had told me to hide in the wagon. I could hear the horrible din of the battle, the guns firing and the Indians yelling.

"Suddenly it was quiet. I heard voices. An Indian jumped on the wagon where I was and threw open the curtain. He flung the covers off the bed, grabbed me under my arms and pulled me onto the ground, enraged that I had been hiding. Then I saw him take out his tomahawk. He slammed it into my chest. He missed my heart and I was still alive, but I could hardly breathe. He hit me again with the tomahawk, this time in the forehead, and then I was out of my body.

"The other Indians came racing up to him. 'Why did you kill her?' they shouted, furious. 'Our instructions were not to kill any women or children!' The other braves punched him in the chest because they were so aggravated with him. 'You're going to be disgraced in front of the whole tribe tonight,' they said, tying his hands behind his back.

"Then the angels came to take me away. I tried to stop them, saying, 'I can't go yet. I have to forgive that man. He killed me in anger. He didn't even know me. I have to tell him I forgive him.' The angels said, 'You can't do that now. You have to come with us.'

"On another day the angels did bring me back, not to the wagons but to the Indian camp. I headed for a tepee on top of a little hill. It had steam coming out of it, and I realized that it was a sweat lodge. The Indian who had killed me was in there so he could have a vision and show remorse for what he had done.

"As I floated in, he looked up, recognized me and started screaming. He was shaking all over. 'Don't kill me! Don't kill me!' he kept shouting. I told him to be quiet. 'I'm not going to kill you,' I said. 'I want to tell you something—I forgive you for killing me.' He said he didn't believe me and started screaming again.

"'You have to promise me that you will not fight any more,' I said. 'I can't promise that,' he replied. 'I'm a brave.' I told him that he had to ask if he could stay behind and protect the women, the old people and the little children. He finally decided he would do that. As I was leaving, the chief and others were racing up to the lodge to see why he had been screaming. That was what I saw, and the moment I forgave him my cough was gone."

Donna had this experience four years ago, and her chronic cough has never returned. She says that revisiting the scene and consciously affirming her forgiveness of the Indian is what sparked her healing. She now thinks that the Indian warrior in that life is now embodied as her former husband. Her husband used to get very angry with her. She remembers that once, in front of their children and a guest, he held a chair over his head, ready to strike her with it. Donna calmly told him to put down the chair and he did.

Since their divorce thirty years ago, Donna has only seen her ex-husband on rare occasions. Recently, however, they met at a family wedding and he treated her much differently than ever before. In fact, he seemed ecstatic to see her. Donna believes that was because his soul sensed that she had fully forgiven him for the violence of that former life and now he was at peace.

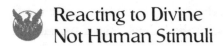

Reacting to Divine Not Human Stimuli

*The only safe reaction to external affairs
is to act on inspiration from on high
and from within.*

—KUTHUMI LAL SINGH

We have become a nation of reactors, Mark Prophet once lamented in his commonsense way. "We are creatures of conditioned response," he said. "Someone pulls the string and we dance. We love those who love us, and we probably do not love those who do not love us. But this is not the way our Father in heaven intended us to be.

"When you are driving your car and you're behaving yourself like a lady or gentleman, and then someone cuts right in front of you and breaks the law with utter disregard, what happens to your temper? In many cases it's like a bulging thermometer. The top of your head is almost ready to pop off, because this person has done something to which you are going to react. This puts them in the driver's seat. They are your master and you are their slave.

"For every cause there is an effect. This we must learn. And we must learn to control ourselves so that we are the reactor to God rather than the reactor to man. We must respond to divine stimuli, not to human stimuli. We must love those that do not love us. We must understand and be compassionate to those who despise us."

Richard learned how important it was to examine his reactions after he had a past-life memory that impelled him to probe the roots of his discontent. Since his college days, Richard had back problems. One night he had a dream where he saw himself dressed in an army uniform during World War II. He was washing himself in the morning outside a farmhouse when suddenly someone hiding in the tall grass behind him took aim and shot him in the back. He awoke with a start and had the sense that his back pain was related to this wound.

Fifteen years later, he uncovered the next layer of the memory. Richard came into work one day to find out that the company where he had worked for years was being downsized and his job had been cut. He felt betrayed, especially by Warren, one of the key people responsible for the cuts.

When he had first met Warren, Richard felt a close tie to him, as if he had known him before. Richard was devastated by the news. For him, it wasn't just his job that was being eliminated; he felt that he was personally being "axed."

Richard took advantage of some work-related counseling from a psychologist, and through the process of free association he went back into his World War II memory. He tuned into the fact that he had been in the French Resistance and Warren had been his close friend. The Germans had captured Warren and threatened that if he didn't kill Richard, they would kill him, his wife and his children. It was Warren who had been hiding in the grass. To save his family, Warren had murdered his good friend.

Richard now understood that his intense over-reaction to the downsizing was really a reaction to Warren's betrayal in that World War II scene. In his heart, he could sense how traumatic that event must have been for Warren and therefore he could forgive him.

Eventually Richard realized that the downsizing was a blessing in disguise, as is often the case with major changes in our life. It prodded him to find a job that was more in line with his life's mission, a job that became a stepping-stone for his professional advancement.

He also realized that the job cut, as painful as it was, had spurred him to deal with his issues of self-worth. The loss of his job was just the latest in a long string of events that he perceived as an attack on his worth, when in fact no one could either take away or give him a sense of self-worth except himself. He knew that his soul and his spirit were of supreme worth and that he had to claim that for himself.

Now when Richard is confronted with situations that seem unjust, he is getting better at catching himself. He stops and reminds himself that this is just another opportunity to affirm his self-worth. And he doesn't always run away from the pain like he used to. Instead, he tries to respond to the divine stimuli that is nudging him to look deeper to find the hidden blessing.

The Interplay of Karma and Psychology

*I find the great thing in this world
is not so much where we stand
as in what direction we are moving.*
—OLIVER WENDELL HOLMES SR.

Our psychology and our karma are intricately intertwined. We may try to deal with the issues of our karma, but if we don't resolve the issues in our psychology that are the result of our karma, the same emotional triggers will cause us to act and react in the same old ways, re-creating or even compounding our karmic load.

We develop certain mental and emotional responses based on our experiences in this life, but we also have propensities that derive from our past lives. We may shy away from conflict because we were once caught in a life-and-death struggle, or we may be overly protective of our children because in a past life our children were taken away from us.

Whenever we have formed habits or defense mechanisms, phobias or addictions, our energy tends to flow naturally through the channels we have already carved. It takes determination, know-how and the appropriate tools to re-create new patterns.

If, for instance, we have a problem with over-spending that has emotional roots, we can hire all the financial coaches we want. But until we understand the karmic causes and the attendant psychological issues that compel us to engage in periodic shopping binges, we will never be able to pay off our credit cards. That's why it's often necessary to work with a trained therapist who can help us move through our psychological issues while we also engage in our spiritual practices and take the necessary physical steps that our situation calls for.

How do we know when a situation in our life has a particularly karmic flavor to it? Lucile Yaney, a psychotherapist who believes in reincarnation, says one clue is a pattern of emotional overreaction, including unexplained fears or phobias. "A person may be responding to past situations from this life or other lifetimes when he has a greater reaction than the current reality calls for," says Yaney, who has been counseling for thirty-five years. The current circumstance that triggers the reaction is not nearly as threatening as the past event, she says, but we perceive it and react to it the way we did originally.

For instance, if we were tortured in a past life-time, we might find ourselves in a situation today where we react to criticism as if we are being attacked or tortured. "In a case like this, we might be reticent to speak up," explains Yaney. "We might have an excessive need to please others. We might not be able to take a stand for ourselves when we come under scrutiny. Instead, we would constantly take the position of victim, becoming defensive, shutting down and, in effect, 'dying.'"

Another sign that we may be dealing with past-life issues, says Yaney, is the intensity of our emotional release once we have resolved a situation. "It may be a small thing that we triumph over," she says, "such as confronting someone we have been afraid of. But when we do it, we feel an intense elation. It's as if all the energy we were using to repress past-life memories becomes unblocked and is now available to us."

Although we don't need to know the details of our past lives to successfully work through our karma, we do have to be willing to self-observe and to watch how we react to events. We have to be willing to understand that there are no accidents or coincidences in life. Whatever is before us is there for a reason. Each encounter is our opportunity to bring karma to its highest resolution.

There may be six different ways to deal with a situation and all may accrue some good karma and good feelings, but only one will be the highest resolution for you, and you will sense it. For example, let's say that in a past life your mother was a child you had abandoned. Now your mother is getting older and needs special care.

"Because you abandoned your mother in the past, you will feel strongly compelled to personally care for her while your siblings may not share those same feelings," says Yaney. "Your brothers and sisters may feel fine discharging the duty of care to someone else, even putting her in a good home where she will be properly cared for. In fact, if your siblings had timely contributions to make to the world through their professions, they could actually be doing a disservice to themselves and others by becoming their mother's caretaker."

You would be able to sense your karmic duty by observing how you felt in this situation, says Yaney. Because of your karmic responsibility, you would probably feel strong and energized by personally caring for your mother. In the case of your siblings, whose foremost duties lay elsewhere, they might feel bitter and unfulfilled if they had to assume that job. Thus our duty may be entirely different than someone else's even though we are in the same situation. It all depends on our karmic history. Our job is to use our free will to follow the inner direction that will lead us to the highest choice.

 ## The Role of Compassion

The whole idea of compassion is based on a keen awareness of the interdependence of all these living beings, which are all part of one another and all involved in one another.
—THOMAS MERTON

Compassion is integral to our karmic transformations—compassion not only for ourselves but also for others. When Michael was growing up, he had trouble trusting anybody, including his parents. At fifteen, he decided he wanted to be an emancipated minor. He informed his mother that he had gone to the library to check out what it would take to become legally free of his parents.

Instead of reacting with anger, his mother took a compassionate stance. "I didn't take it personally," she said. "I was very aware of his struggle. I could understand what he must have been going through. So I put my arm around him and said, 'You know, if you had bad parents, that is exactly what you would need to do. But, honey, in this lifetime you were given good parents that do support you and are on your side. We're behind you. You don't need to emancipate yourself from good parents.'"

The next day she overheard her son on the phone explaining to a friend that he had been planning to fill out the forms to become an emancipated minor, but he had figured out that he had really good parents and he didn't need to do that. "All the energy around that situation disappeared," said his mother. "It never came up again." She had the feeling that someone Michael had trusted deeply in a past life had betrayed him. Not until his parents supported him through some tough experiences, where he expected them to abandon him, was he really able to trust them.

Toni also had an issue of trust that was solved

through a different kind of compassion. Ever since Toni could remember, she was uncomfortable around guys. When she was a little girl, she never spent much time with boys. As a young woman, she had her share of boyfriends but always maintained a certain distance.

Toni married relatively late in life. "Though my husband was strong and masculine, he was also very gentle," she says. "Even so, if he would raise his voice even slightly or get a bit irritated, I would get frightened and retreat into myself. Gradually, because of his loving, attentive and protective nature, I began to soften. Still, a part of myself remained unconnected to him. When I wanted to be vulnerable and fully open with him, I wasn't able to. I never understood why."

One day, after being married for over ten years, Toni decided she wanted to find out why she felt the need to put up barriers between herself and men, including her husband. She worked with a counselor who used a technique that allowed Toni to access events from this life and past lives without hypnosis. This is her story in her own words.

"As I closed my eyes and tried to contact my feelings of mistrust, I saw myself as a girl in another lifetime. It was a sunny day and I was playing outside. The world seemed beautiful and good, and I was carefree and happy. I had been playing too long and I knew I would be late for supper. To get home more quickly, I decided to walk through the woods. The sun was already going down and there was a slight chill in the air. As I entered the woods, I felt a bit uneasy. But I kept walking, telling myself that there was nothing to be afraid of.

"Then I sensed that someone was there, not too far away. In the shadows of the approaching nightfall, I could make out the shape of a man. I soon recognized him as someone who worked at my parents' farm. He had always been nice to me, but now there was something strange about him. I didn't want to be near him. I wanted to be safe at home. He came closer and touched me, and everything that followed was in a haze. Blackness covered the whole scene. The next sensation I had was that I was lying in icy swamp water and everything was cold and dark. I was dead. But I remembered my final thoughts: 'I will never again trust a man, and I will never give myself to him.'

"With some coaxing, I went back to the moments when I first recognized who the man was.

I realized that this wasn't the first time he had done this to someone. And yet, I don't think he was actually a mean or bad man. He was just very disturbed. He wasn't in his right mind. To him it was as if someone else, not himself, had hurt me and the others. Understanding this, I was able to have compassion for him and forgive him, and I prayed that he would be healed."

Toni realized that ever since the experience she had in that life, she had believed the lie that she could never trust any man. In that terrible moment, she had made the decision to always withhold a part of herself, even from the one who now loved her most. She understood at last that she could trust men discriminately, depending on the individual—and that she could love and trust her husband without reserve.

"A great burden was lifted from me," says Toni. "After the session, I returned to the arms of my husband, and I could feel the love for him that I always knew was there. My love merged with his. It enveloped us and expanded beyond us both. I learned that if you can understand, have compassion and forgive another, even for what may be a heinous crime, then you can be free to love and be loved."

When we hear stories like this, we tend to think of the poignant issues of our karma and our psychology as stemming from a single outstanding or traumatic event that caused us to mar or scar another or vice versa. Yet it is also the larger pattern of day-to-day influences and our responses to them, in this and past lives, that have created our karma, our character and our psychology.

Psychologists tell us that we are molded by the build-up of our traumas and that the daily pounding of harmful influences, such as criticisms or stinging remarks, can be more detrimental than any one shocking event.

Whatever dramas of the past we carry forward, we are the final arbiters of our destiny. We are not victims. We can approach our soul work from a point of adult responsibility and compassion and say, "Okay, this unfortunate situation existed in my childhood or in a past life, but I am who I am. I am a son, a daughter of God, and I am determining the course of my life. Yes, I may have had a dysfunctional family, but I will send them mercy and forgiveness. My parents and others I have known are responsible for their actions, but I am also responsible for how I react to them.

"I will make certain that I correct those elements in myself that have caused me to create negative karma, and I will make sure that I give my own children and those I meet along life's way a better opportunity to become who they are. In the process of experimenting in the laboratory of self, I may make mistakes, but I will not criticize myself. I will learn from those mistakes and move forward. And I will not forget to love myself and to celebrate those elements within me that have helped me to create good karma."

The Gold in the Mud

*Journey from self to Self
and find the mine of gold.* —RUMI

Someone once gave me profound advice when I felt I had made the worst decision of my life. The advice was: you learn more from a wrong decision than a right one. As James Joyce once wrote, "Mistakes are the portals of discovery." Yet many of us are unforgiving when it comes to our own mistakes or errors in judgment. We can't seem to forgive ourselves for not meeting the illusive and slippery standard of "perfection."

Robert Kennedy once pointed out that "only those who dare to fail greatly can ever achieve greatly." On this daring adventure we call life, we are inevitably going to make a wrong turn here or there. That doesn't make us any less valuable. It is necessary to contact the pain we may have caused others through our mistakes. It is necessary to feel, with the full sensitivity of our heart, the remorse that convinces our soul never to hurt another part of life like that again. But it is also necessary to get over it. Guilt is the enemy of growth.

No matter what mistakes we've made, we were doing the best we could at the time. Now it's time to forgive ourselves, to get on with our life and to keep our eye focused on the vast spiritual potential we have inside of us. Therein lies the crux of the issue. We all have that vast spiritual potential, but we don't always accept it, especially when others belittle us or we belittle ourselves.

To make it through the everyday initiations of our karma, we need not only a higher perspective of the situation but also an inner perspective of our own divine reality. We need to affirm and reaffirm the gold that shines at the very core of our identity.

Both the Buddhists and the Christian Gnostics used the image of the "gold in the mud" to help us understand our spiritual essence. They said that the gold of our spirit may be covered over by the mud of the world, but the mud never destroys the beauty of that innate spirit.

Buddhism teaches that each of us contains the germ, or seed, of the Buddha, and that therefore we are all Buddhas in the making. The Buddhist text *Uttaratantra* explains this truth with the following analogy: "The Germ of the Buddha has a resemblance with gold. Suppose that the gold belonging to a certain man was, at the time of his departure, cast into a place filled with impurities. Being of an indestructible nature, this gold would remain there for many hundreds of years." The text goes on to say that "the Lord perceives the true virtues [the "gold"] of the living beings sunk amidst the passions that are like impurities." In order to "wash off this dirt," the Buddha lets the rain of the highest teaching descend on all that lives.

The Gnostics also spoke of our golden nature. According to the second-century Greek Church Father Irenaeus, the Gnostics taught that our "spiritual substance" could not be corrupted, just as "gold, when submersed in filth," does not lose its beauty but "retains its own native qualities, the filth having no power to injure the gold."

In other words, it doesn't matter what you've been through. It doesn't matter how much mud (karma) has splattered onto your soul and shaped your outer personality on the road of life. It doesn't matter what other people say about you. You are still a child of God—pure gold. You are capable of that grand spiritual adventure that is your birthright. And the pilot of that journey is your Higher Self.

Your Higher Self is part of your treasury of

gold. Your Higher Self is your innate higher consciousness and guiding light, your wise inner teacher
and dearest friend. Jesus discovered that Higher Self
to be "the Christ" and Gautama discovered it to be
"the Buddha." Thus that Higher Self is also called
the inner Christ (or Christ Self) as well as the inner
Buddha. The Hindus refer to our Higher Self as the
Atman and Christian mystics sometimes call it the
Inner Light or the inner man of the heart.

When we are in the midst of a difficult situation, our Higher Self is our greatest ally and
teacher. We can consciously go into our heart,
which is the seat of our higher consciousness, and
attune with the inner voice of wisdom that flows
from our Higher Self. We can ask our Higher Self
to show us the spiritual dynamics that are at play
in any circumstance, what steps we must take to
resolve our karmic challenges, and how day by day
we can make the most of our good karma.

The Grace of Good Karma

One cannot escape from the effect of one's past karma. But if a person lives a prayerful life, he gets off with only the prick of a thorn in the leg where he was to suffer from a deep cut.

—SRI SARADA DEVI

Sometimes the momentum of our good karma brings us what we call "grace"—a break that we didn't expect but we sorely need. The Indian master and teacher Paramahansa Yogananda relates a story about the master Babaji that describes how grace can work.

One night, Babaji's disciples were sitting around a bonfire that had been prepared for a sacred ceremony. Suddenly Babaji grabbed a burning brand from the hot fire and lightly struck the bare shoulder of a disciple who was near the fire. "How cruel!" exclaimed one of the master's disciples. But Babaji responded, "Would you rather have seen him burned to ashes before your eyes, according to the decree of his past karma?" Then the master put his hand on the disciple's injured shoulder and healed him, saying, "I have freed you tonight from painful death. The karmic law has been satisfied through your slight suffering by fire."[1]

We've all seen the good karma of grace in action. Take these recent examples. While Jan was hiking in the mountains, she took a bad fall and hit her head hard against a rock. Fortunately her hiking buddy used to teach first aid and knew exactly what to do. When two tourists overturned their car, the first person on the scene was an emergency medical technician, who was driving by with his family. If you have to deal with returning karma, what better way than to have the immediate help and comfort that your good karma affords?

Rob, whose three-and-a-half-year-old daughter was diagnosed recently with leukemia, marvels that both he and his wife were able to help diagnose her disease before it became a life-and-death situation. His wife had been a nurse and he had helped research leukemia treatments during summers as a premed student, even though he never pursued medicine as a career.

"It's amazing to me how my daughter was born to two parents who would recognize her vague but life-threatening symptoms in time," says Rob. "Our past medical experience also took away some of the shock most parents feel in this kind of situation, and we're well prepared to run a small 'clinic' at home during the next two years of her care and treatment."

While Rob and his wife were in the children's hospital where their daughter stayed during the first days of her emergency care, Rob commented to one doctor that he and his wife had discussed leukemia as a possible source of his little girl's distressing symptoms a month before her actual diagnosis. "Many of the parents or relatives of children diagnosed with leukemia are actually nurses or are in the medical profession," the doctor told him. God's grace in action.

I, too, learned something about the nature of returning karma and grace when I was a college student at Boston University. The example may seem minor, but the impact of the lesson was lasting. I was hurrying out the door of my dorm when I heard an inner voice tell me to put on my heavy winter coat and gloves. It was a beautiful spring day, so I thought to myself, "This is the craziest thing I've ever heard of. Okay, I'll put on the coat but not these heavy gloves. It's just too hot!"

So I threw on my coat and ran down the street

so I wouldn't be late for my class. I crossed a street between some cars that were stopped at a light and *bam!* A bicycle came speeding alongside one of the cars, ran right into me and knocked me to the ground. I caught myself on my bare hands. The fur-lined coat insulated my body but my hands were scraped. If I had put on my gloves, I wouldn't have had a scratch.

There is a time and space where we converge with forces we have set in motion in the past—our karma—and that's exactly what happened to me that day. My Higher Self had tried to mitigate that karma by giving me a direction. But my stubborn reasoning mind was not able to accept it, so I lost the full benefit of the blessing, although I certainly didn't lose the lesson.

Another factor in mitigating karma is that karma takes time to cycle into the physical. First it passes through the etheric, mental and emotional planes of being. So before it hits the physical—before the fruit of our karma becomes fully ripened—we have time to either slow down or mitigate the result. For instance, before disease becomes a physical reality, we may be able to turn it back if we resolve the emotional or karmic causes behind it.

There are other possibilities of grace. As we saw in the story of Babaji and his disciple, we may merit some kind of dispensation whereby we receive only a token of the full karma that was originally slated. We may be allowed to balance a certain karma in some other way than being crushed by it. Or we may be given an extension of time before the karma comes due.

Say someone's karma dictates that he meet with a certain setback or calamity at age forty-nine. The Karmic Board, that group of spiritual overseers we spoke of in part 3, may make an adjustment based on his sincerity, his good works and the light he has garnered through his spiritual practice. They may decide that the karma will not come due for another ten years so that he has more time to spend with his young children or to develop his spiritual gifts.

Grace, however, doesn't mean that our past transgressions are erased altogether. Just as the concept of forgiveness has been misunderstood, so has the concept of grace. Advanced spiritual beings, like Jesus, Gautama Buddha, Kuan Yin or Mary, can and do intercede for their devotees so that karma can be held in abeyance. But that doesn't excuse us from our accountability. The extension gives us time to grow stronger and become better prepared to gracefully deal with our karma when it finally lands on our doorstep.

Unfortunately, many of us have grown up with a fundamental misunderstanding of the principle of grace based on what we were taught about Jesus. Jesus has indeed played a special role. He was and is the great spiritual master chosen to incarnate as the sponsor of the Piscean age. His mission was to demonstrate how to become the fullness of "the Christ" (another term for the Higher Self, or the "Son") so that we, too, would know how to become one with our own Higher Self. That is the real role of a "Saviour"—one who is empowered to help us reconnect with our Source, not one who replaces our connection with that Source.

In his role, Jesus did bear the weight of the negative karma, or "sins," of the world for the past two thousand years. That means he shielded us from the full consequences of our misdeeds. In essence, he gave us a kind of reprieve. He volunteered to help carry the weight of our karma until we were strong enough to bear it ourselves.

In the course of earth's history, other adepts East and West have also held in abeyance mankind's negative karma for thousands of years by their spiritual consciousness. This does not mean they canceled the debt; they only postponed our payment of it. As we move from the age of Pisces into the age of Aquarius in this new millennium, we must now face our karma. Every one of us must assume the responsibility of bearing our own burden. It's a time when we are called to demonstrate our spiritual maturity.

During this period of karmic summing up, we can all expect the harvest of good karma as well as negative karma, personal karma as well as group karma. This is why so many of us are seeing and feeling an acceleration in our lives. There seems to be more to deal with in even less time, and the stakes seem to be getting higher. Yet as never before, we have the spiritual tools and techniques to successfully navigate the karmic straits on our voyage of self-discovery.

 A Proactive Approach

Even if you're on the right track,
you'll get run over if you just sit there.
—WILL ROGERS

We can go through life letting the rough seas take us where they will, or we can learn how to maneuver through the unexpected storms and navigate safely to our destination. We can allow the wind to sweep us this way and that, or we can learn how to turn the wind to our advantage. It's a matter of being proactive and self-directed.

On the path of spiritual transformation, we have to be willing to explore. Are you willing to contemplate the paradoxes? To observe your reactions to events? To listen to the message that lies hidden within the folds of every challenge? Are you willing to ask yourself—your Higher Self—some penetrating questions and then listen to the answers?

This kind of exploration can help us follow the karmic threads back to the origin of our difficulties. It can help us identify karmic traps. Self-reflection can take us to a higher perspective—a perspective we sorely need, since many times we react not to the outer circumstance but to what that circumstance reminds us of. Looking beyond the actors and actions to the inner drama and the karmic context can help us depersonalize and take the sting out of an issue.

After all, neither life nor the path of resolution is a "who done it" affair. The person who seems to have hurt us may be the instrument of our karma, showing us where we have not acted with love in the past. He may be playing his assigned part so that we can learn something about ourselves that we never knew before. We don't have to condone that one's actions, but we can bless the carrier of the message, send him love, and then take a look within to see if there is anything new to learn.

Here are some key questions that can help you navigate on your journey of self-transformation. These are the kinds of questions you can return to time and again when you feel stuck or have a sense that there is a higher resolution to be gleaned.

For reflection on the messengers and the message

- Who or what are the messengers of my karma right now?

- What am I supposed to learn from being in this situation?
- What is the pain or discomfort trying to teach me?
- What am I supposed to give?
- Is there someone I must forgive, including myself?

For reflection on my reactions

- Are my reactions appropriate to the circumstance or do I overreact?
- What caused me to react the way I did?
- When have I been in a similar circumstance or felt the way I am feeling now?
- Was this reaction part of a pattern I have?
- How can I give a more compassionate response—to myself and to others?

For reflection on my responsibility

- What habit of mine caused this incident to take place?
- How am I responsible?
- Is there something I am avoiding facing about myself?

- Where have I allowed my energy and my
  attention to be tied up in negative habit
  patterns?

For reflection on the next steps

- What must I do to turn this challenge
  into an opportunity?
- What techniques from my spiritual
  toolbox can I apply to this situation?
- What positive behaviors and attitudes do
  I need to develop so that when this karmic
  challenge knocks again at my door I can
  resolve the karma with integrity?
- Is there anyone who can help coach me
  through this?
- What is the next assignment of my karma?
- What should I be focusing on right now?

For reflection on the highest good

- How can I take full advantage of my good
  karma, in the form of my good qualities
  and talents, to help resolve my challenges?
- What is the highest resolution that can
  come out of this situation?

A Map of Our Karma

> *A child is born on that day and at that hour
> when the celestial rays are in mathematical
> harmony with his individual karma.*
>
> —SRI YUKTESWAR

Another tool we can use to work with our karma is astrology. Astrology is a map of karma. Your birth chart tells you the positive karma (in the form of talents, attainments and blessings) and the negative karma (in the form of challenges and obstacles) you are bringing with you from your past lives. It tells you the good momentums you can count on as the wind in your sails as well as what are the lessons you will have to learn in this life.

For some, astrology has become a superstitious and superficial plaything, but when properly interpreted this ancient and profound science can tell us when to anticipate cycles of good karma, when to anticipate periods of karmic challenges, and what form they are likely to take. You can also chart the ongoing cycles of your returning karma through a system of spiritual astrology known as the science of the cosmic clock.[2]

Yogananda in his *Autobiography of a Yogi* recounts that his teacher, Sri Yukteswar, taught him that just because the ignorant and the charlatans "have brought the ancient stellar science [of astrology] to its present disrepute," it does not mean that it isn't a profound discipline. "All parts of creation are linked together and interchange their influences," he said. "The balanced rhythm of the universe is rooted in reciprocity."

But astrology, like karma, is not predestination. Astrology paints a picture of potentials based on the karmic material drawn from our many appearances on the stage of life. Our astrology and our karma are only part of the drama. At center stage is our free will. Man, said Sri Yukteswar, "can overcome any limitation, because he created it by his own actions in the first place, and because he possesses spiritual resources that are not subject to planetary pressure."[3]

How will we react to the chemistry of our returning karma? Will we accept responsibility and learn the lessons of the past? Or will we fall back into the same patterns? How we answer those questions will determine our destiny, not the configurations in the skies.

The Power of Heart and Hand

True spirituality, as taught in our sacred lore, is calmly balanced in strength, in the correlation of the within and the without.

—RABINDRANATH TAGORE

Not all karma is created equally or balanced equally. At times we may be required to balance our karma by directly interacting with those we have made karma with in the past. Sometimes we can work through our karma by facing the same challenges that we didn't resolve last time around but we can do it in a different setting. In other cases, we may have to bear a burden for a time in our body, our mind or our emotions because we have placed that burden upon others in the past.

Whether or not the world's spiritual traditions embrace reincarnation and karma, they all have spiritual practices for balancing karma—from Christianity's penance or atonement for sin to Judaism's performing of mitzvahs (good deeds) to Buddhism's Eightfold Path.

Spiritual practices for resolving karma involve everything from serving others to fasting, prayer and other accelerated techniques of spiritual cleansing. They involve our heart, our head and our hands. We have made karma with our heart, head and hands and we can balance that karma in exactly the same way.

Our "hands" represent our actions. Our everyday actions or nonactions, including how we express ourselves through our profession, are a tremendous factor in balancing karma. No matter what our calling or profession, our work is part of our spiritual path, and from time to time we must ask ourselves: Does the work of my hands serve society and enhance the quality of life of those who come within the sphere of my influence?

When we get right down to it, how we physically work with our karma isn't complex. We start by addressing the need that is right in front of us rather than turning a blind eye because it doesn't seem to fit into our schedule. Just look around you. If the floor is dirty, scrub it. If the dishes have to be done, wash them. If someone needs to be nursed, nurse them. If someone in your family just lost their job and you are in a position to lend them support, open your heart and give. "The giving of self," says the adept Djwal Kul, is what "propels you to transmute karma and to move on in the cycles of being." Wherever you are, look at the need and meet it.

We also balance karma through the activity of the heart. How have we made karma at the level of the heart? Through every self-centered moment that deprives someone else of God's love. Anytime we are self-centered and therefore not generous, cold and therefore not comforting, insensitive and therefore not compassionate, we create a karma of the heart. We can balance that karma as we exercise the healing power of love.

Balancing karma through the heart means opening the heart and giving wisely. It means not being afraid to pour out more love, even when that love may be rejected. That love is never rejected by God. This realization has helped me to see all kinds of relationships as learning experiences and as opportunities to give more love, even if I am rebuffed.

One time, seemingly by chance, I unexpectedly met someone I hadn't seen for years. I realized that the last time I had seen him I could have spoken to him in a better way and I wanted to apologize. So

I put out my hand to shake his hand. "I'm not going to shake your hand," he said angrily. "Well, I want you to know that I love you," I replied. "And I need to love you." In a sense, you could say that took some courage, and it did. But it was what my soul needed to do at the time.

I could only do my best and trust in God to do the rest. I also knew that my love was not wasted, even if this person didn't seem to accept it. The truth is that he also needed that love at some level of his being, whether he realized it or not.

When we are in pain because our love seems to be rejected, we can ask God to bless the one we have loved, to help that person become more of his true self, and to heal both of us of the hurts of the past. You can also ask God to help you understand why you are hurting, because that's where the lesson comes in.

Sometimes people get the idea that paying off karmic debts is like walking the via dolorosa, the sorrowful way. It doesn't have to be. How do you feel when at long last you can pay off your credit card bill? Paying off your karmic debts feels just as good. It's a joy to be able to embrace the one we may have hurt and to reestablish the harmony and love that is native to our souls.

In fact, when we have fully integrated with the law of karma as the law of love, we find that we are no longer motivated to do good works just to balance our own karmic debts or to create good karma—or because it was what we were taught to do so we could get to heaven. We serve those who are suffering simply because they need us. We give from our heart without a second thought because we love every part of life as a part of God. At the end of the day, it's the quality of our heart and how much love we have given that will make all the difference.

Mental Matrices

The mind is its own place, and in itself
Can make a heav'n of hell, a hell of heav'n.

—JOHN MILTON

We can also make karma and balance it by the way we use our mind. We make good karma when we use our thoughts and our knowledge to help, uplift and teach others. We misuse the potential of our mind when we criticize or control rather than uphold, when we are narrow-minded or prejudiced instead of tolerant, when we compete with our knowledge rather than share it.

Our mind can be the conduit for the consciousness of our Higher Self or for the pride of the ego. In either case, our thoughts are a powerful force. "We are what we think," said Gautama Buddha, "having become what we thought."

We can balance karma at the level of the mind when we hold in mind the highest image, the "immaculate concept," of ourselves and others. Holding in mind the immaculate concept means that we don't jump to conclusions before we know the facts. Rather than holding fixed mental matrices of others, we allow them to transcend what they were decades ago, weeks ago or even an hour ago. Our thoughts are so powerful that when we consistently hold in mind the highest vision of good for ourselves and others, we can literally create what we are seeing in our mind's eye.

A change in heart (and mind) by author Peter Benchley is an interesting example of how we might balance the karma we make in the realm of the mind. Almost twenty-five years ago, Benchley's novel *Jaws,* which spent more than forty weeks on the *New York Times* best-sellers list, was made into the hit movie. That savage image of the great white shark has been seared into the consciousness of millions. Now Benchley is offering another viewpoint.

In a recent *National Geographic* article, he wrote, "Considering the knowledge accumulated about great whites in the past 25 years, I couldn't possibly write *Jaws* today... not in good conscience anyway." He points out that while we once thought that the great white sharks ruthlessly hunted down humans, we now know they only kill and eat when they mistake a human for their normal prey. We used to think they attacked boats, but we now know that when they approach a boat they are just investigating. True, these sharks can slash and kill when provoked, but we now know that they are also fragile and vulnerable.

Benchley says that these awesome animals "are not only *not* villains, they are victims in danger of —if not extinction quite yet—serious, perhaps even catastrophic, decline." Perhaps Benchley is balancing some karma with the great whites by now portraying them in a different light. How can we learn from this? We have all influenced how others think. And if we have influenced them negatively, we can balance that karma by correcting wrong, misleading or incomplete information we have spread—whether to one person or to thousands.

 ## Spiritual Alchemy

Where there is fire, there is evidence of progressive perfection.

—HELENA ROERICH

The masters of the ancient Oriental art of Feng Shui teach that clutter in our physical environment inhibits the flow of energy, or ch'i, in our surroundings. They say that the flow of energy (or lack of it) powerfully affects our health, our finances, our relationships—the very course of our life.

In exactly the same way, "karmic clutter" can create blockages in the flow of energy at subtle, energetic levels within us. These blockages of accumulated unresolved karma affect our physical and emotional well-being, our spiritual progress, even the kinds of events and people that move in and out of our life. When energy flows freely, we feel peaceful, healthy and creative. When it is blocked, we don't feel as light, vibrant and spiritual as we could.

Just as we wash off the dirt and grime we pick up every day, so we can have a daily ritual of purifying to free ourselves of karmic debris. Each spiritual tradition has its particular practices for purification. Many of these are sacred formulas of prayer and meditation that call forth the light of the Holy Spirit to purify the heart.

In some traditions, this powerfully transforming energy of the Holy Spirit has been seen as a violet light, known as the violet flame. Just as a ray of sunlight passing through a prism is refracted into the seven colors of the rainbow, so spiritual light manifests as seven rays, or flames. When we call forth these spiritual flames in our prayers and meditations, each flame creates a specific action in our body, mind and soul. The violet flame is the color and frequency of spiritual light that stimulates mercy, forgiveness and transmutation.

To "transmute" is to change something into a higher form. This term was used centuries ago by alchemists who attempted, on a physical level, to transmute base metals into gold—and, on a spiritual level, to achieve self-transformation and ultimately eternal life. Spiritually, that is precisely what the violet flame can do. It is a high-frequency spiritual energy that separates the "gross" elements of our karma from the gold of our true self and transmutes (transforms) it so we can achieve our highest potential.

Healers, alchemists and adepts have used the high-frequency energy of the violet flame to bring about energetic balance and spiritual transformation. Edgar Cayce, for instance, recognized the healing power of the violet light. In over nine hundred of his readings, he recommended an electrical device—a "violet ray" machine that emits a violet-colored electrical charge—to treat several ailments, including exhaustion, lethargy, poor circulation, digestive problems and nervous disorders.

Author and three-time near-death survivor Dannion Brinkley has seen and experienced the violet flame in his near-death sojourns. "The violet flame is the purest place of love. It's what really empowers you," he says. "The violet flame is a light that serves all spiritual heritages, that gives respect and dignity to all things. It gives us a way to connect with each other. . . . The greatness of the violet flame is that it doesn't produce heat; it produces love."

What makes the violet flame such a powerful tool? In our physical world, violet light has the highest frequency in the visible spectrum. As Fritjof Capra explains in *The Tao of Physics,* "violet light has a high frequency and a short wavelength and consists therefore of photons of high energy and high momentum."[4] At spiritual levels, that high-frequency energy of the violet flame can consume the debris within and between the atoms of your being. It's like soaking them in a chemical solution that, layer by layer, dissolves the dirt that has been trapped there for years.

Freed of this dross, the electrons begin to move more freely, thus raising our spiritual vibration and our energy levels. This action takes place at non-physical, or "metaphysical," dimensions of matter. As energy is repolarized and transmuted, it becomes part of our storehouse of positive energy.

There is not one of us that doesn't regret some moment of our life, some action, some unkind word. We wish we could call it back. By working with the violet flame, we can send the flame of the Holy Spirit to deliver the one we have wronged as well as ourselves of the burden. As the violet flame passes through the emotional, mental and physical layers of our being, it transmutes the cause, effect, record and memory of anything less than perfection and restores that energy back to its natural state of harmony with Spirit.

In essence, the violet flame affords us a path of minimum suffering. When we call forth that light through our prayers, it can help ease the process of resolving karma and trauma. It can even enable us to balance some of our karmic debts without directly encountering those involved. The violet flame, like the flames that consume the phoenix, is a sacred fire that helps us rise again renewed, refreshed and more whole.

 ## A Sacred Fire

Our God is a consuming fire.
—THE BOOK OF HEBREWS

The phoenix is far more than a symbol of rebirth. It also represents self-transcendence and self-transformation. The fire that at once consumes and rejuvenates the phoenix is the same fire that purifies us for a better resurrection, so to speak.

The German philosopher Hegel captured the true nature of the phoenix when he wrote, "Spirit

—consuming the envelope of its existence—does not merely pass into another envelope, nor rise rejuvenescent from the ashes of its previous form; it comes forth exalted, glorified, a purer spirit. . . . It exalts itself to a new grade." [5]

The phoenix is you, every day, meeting the trial by fire of your returning karma with the fire of your heart and the sacred fire of the violet flame. It is you going through the process of growth and refinement, continually surpassing your former self. The apostle Paul described it another way when he said, "I die daily." When we are dedicated to spiritual growth, some part of our lesser self can "die daily," clearing the way for more of our Higher Self to come to the fore and express itself.

We can get in touch with the gentle power of the violet flame through prayer, meditation and affirmation. Those who have accessed the violet flame in their prayers and meditations have found that it helps them move safely through the sometimes painful records of the past. One woman wrote to me and said, "For years I had consulted with psychologists. They had helped me to see causes, but how could I change?" She started working with violet-flame prayers every day and said that the violet flame penetrated and dissolved core resentment. "Through the violet flame," she said, "I emerged healthy, vigorous and grateful."

If you are aware of a particular issue, such as anxiety that doesn't seem to have roots in this life, you can ask God or your Higher Self to direct the violet flame into the roots of that anxiety in your previous embodiments and to restore that energy to its pure state. You can use the alchemy of the violet flame to clear the subconscious, which often accepts the intimidation and judgment of peers and authority figures. The violet flame can help resolve these patterns of consciousness and free us to be more of our real self.

I've seen thousands of people work successfully with the violet flame. It takes a different amount of time—anywhere from a day to several months—for each person to see results, depending on the intensity of the issue, event or pattern you are dealing with. But if you remain constant, you will begin to feel the difference.

When we use the violet flame consistently, memories from this life or past lives may come to the fore. This is because the Holy Spirit is going into our subconscious to consume the cause, effect and memory of that record. When this happens, it's best not to get emotionally involved or to block it. Just let it pass into the light.

When God brings to our attention a record of our childhood or a past life, it's a reminder that there is work to be done. He doesn't reveal it to us for entertainment but so that we can pass the light through it and move beyond it.

Someone who had been working with violet-flame affirmations for some time wrote and told me that it helped her become aware of a key past life. She said, "One morning as I woke up, I had a distinct feeling that something was different. I didn't know what, but things just felt different. As I went to the bathroom and looked in the mirror, I felt I even looked different. There was not necessarily a physical difference but perhaps a difference in my aura. Something was definitely changed.

"I thought to myself, 'What is different? Why do I feel this way?' Then a thought came to me, like a still small voice: 'Yes, I am different, and it is because I have started to transmute the karma from another life.'

"As the morning went on and I was sitting at my desk, suddenly a scene of a past life flashed before my eyes. It was a picture of me—a little different, but definitely me. I was aware of my feelings, my state of consciousness, my life at that time. It was a life on Atlantis and, as in this life, I was a woman. I had a high position in the government as a minister or official of some kind with a lot of power. I realized that I liked having power over people and using that power for my own ends. I had a huge ego.

"I had seen a part of myself face-to-face. It was not something I was aware of before. I am grateful that it was shown to me and I am grateful for the opportunity to work through this with the fire of God and the violet flame. I didn't even have to be hypnotically regressed. God showed it to me in his time, when I was ready and able to see it for what it was and when I could give the prayers to change it." After this woman became aware of this past life, she began to give violet-flame prayers and meditations to balance the karma she had made in that embodiment and to dissolve any remaining threads of egotism within her that would hold her back in this life.

We are entering a new age, which affords us creative ways of balancing personal and planetary karma, and the violet flame is one of them. The violet flame gives us the maximum opportunity to take advantage of the cycles of life and the cycles of karma. As we do our spiritual work and engage in the practical hands-on service that is required to balance our karma, we realize that every day is a tremendous opportunity to transcend our past and transform our tomorrows.

 ## Prayers and Affirmations

More things are wrought by prayer
Than this world dreams of.
Wherefore, let thy voice
Rise like a fountain.

—ALFRED, LORD TENNYSON

We invite you to experiment with any or all of the prayers and affirmations on the following pages to enhance your own spiritual practice and path of karmic transformation. You can give them aloud every day and especially when you feel a burden or heaviness.

I always encourage those who are new to the violet flame to begin their experiment in the laboratory of being by giving violet-flame prayers and affirmations fifteen minutes a day for at least a month. You can give these affirmations during your morning prayer ritual, while you're in the shower or getting ready for the day, or even as you travel to work, do your errands or exercise. Since our karma for the day arrives each morning seeking resolution, many like to give violet-flame prayers and affirmations before their day begins.

The following affirmations use the name of God "I AM" to access spiritual power. "I AM" is short for "I AM THAT I AM," the name of God revealed to Moses when he saw the burning bush. "I AM THAT I AM" means "As above, so below. As God is in heaven, so God is on earth within me. Right where I stand, the power of God is." Thus every time you say, "*I AM*...," you are really affirming "*God in me is....*"

As you experiment with these techniques, keep in mind two key principles. First, these affirmations are intended to be given aloud. Ancient spiritual traditions as well as modern scientific studies have shown how powerful sound is in creating change, even healing. Secondly, we can enhance the power of our prayers when we specifically name and visualize what we want to take place. That's because whatever we put our attention on, we are plugging into and charging with energy. The image we hold in our mind's eye is like a blueprint, and our attention is the magnet that attracts the creative energies of Spirit to fill it in.[6]

Suggested visualizations

While saying these violet-flame affirmations aloud, you can visualize the exact outcome you are praying for as if it were already taking place in the present. See it as if it were happening on a movie screen in front of you. If you don't have a specific outcome in mind, you can concentrate on the words of the prayer and see the action they describe taking place before you.

In addition, you can visualize the violet flame penetrating in, through and around people, events and issues you are praying for. See dancing violet flames consuming negative karma and habit patterns that hinder you or those you pray for. See violet-colored flames within your heart and the hearts of those involved, softening and then melting away any hardness of heart—transforming anger into compassion, bitterness into sweetness, anxiety into peace.

The Violet-Flame Mantra

An easy affirmation to start with is *"I AM a being of violet fire, I AM the purity God desires!"* It is meant to be repeated over and over as a mantra that sings in your heart. The more you give it, the stronger the action of transmutation you are building. You can recite any of the affirmations on the following pages once, three times or as many times as you want until you feel your heart responding to the healing power of love that comes through the violet flame.

> *I AM a being of violet fire*
> *I AM the purity God desires* *
>
> *My heart is alive with violet fire,*
> *My heart is the purity God desires!*
>
> *My family is enfolded in violet fire,*
> *My family is the purity God desires!*

---

*You can create your own variations of the mantra wherever you perceive the need for a higher resolution in any situation, as shown in the two examples below this mantra.

Energizing Heart, Head and Hand

You can use the following affirmations to transmute the karma you have made with your heart, head and hands. This series ends with a prayer for the protective white light, which you can visualize around yourself, as shown on page 135.

Heart

Violet fire, thou love divine,
Blaze within this heart of mine!
Thou art mercy forever true,
Keep me always in tune with you.

Head

I AM light, thou Christ in me,
Set my mind forever free;
Violet fire, forever shine
Deep within this mind of mine.

God who gives my daily bread,
With violet fire fill my head
Till thy radiance heavenlike
Makes my mind a mind of light.

Hand

I AM the hand of God in action,
Gaining victory every day;
My pure soul's great satisfaction
Is to walk the Middle Way.

Tube of Light

Beloved I AM Presence bright,
Round me seal your tube of light
From ascended master flame
Called forth now in God's own name.
Let it keep my temple free
From all discord sent to me.

I AM calling forth violet fire
To blaze and transmute all desire,
Keeping on in freedom's name
Till I AM one with the violet flame.

Affirmation for Forgiveness

Before giving the following affirmations, you can offer this prayer or your own personal prayer aloud:

> *In the name of the I AM THAT I AM and my Higher Self, my inner Christ and my inner Buddha, I call on the law of forgiveness for all that I have ever done in any of my lifetimes that has hurt any part of life—anything that was not kind, loving, respectful or honorable, especially _____.*
>
> *I call forth the violet transmuting flame on behalf of all those whom I have ever wronged and all those who have ever wronged me. I ask for a flow of light and love from my Higher Self and my heart to bless all life with whom I have karma. O God, liberate them, liberate me, and let us stand free, one in heart and soul.*
>
> *Let the violet flame heal my inner pain and transmute the cause, effect, record and memory of all burdens I have ever imposed upon life or that have ever been imposed*

upon me, back to my first incarnation. I surrender them into the light.

Let this sacred fire purify and rejuvenate
my heart, mind, body and soul. Let it restore
them to the harmony and perfection of my
divine blueprint so that I may joyfully fulfill
my soul's true potential. I accept this done in
full power, according to God's will.

Forgiveness

I AM *forgiveness acting here,*
Casting out all doubt and fear,
Setting men forever free
With wings of cosmic victory.

I AM *calling in full power*
For forgiveness every hour;
To all life in every place
I flood forth forgiving grace.

I AM the Violet Flame

I AM the violet flame
  In action in me now
I AM the violet flame
  To light alone I bow
I AM the violet flame
  In mighty cosmic power
I AM the light of God
  Shining every hour
I AM the violet flame
  Blazing like a sun
I AM God's sacred power
  Freeing every one

Prayer for World Peace

Through our heartfelt prayers and meditations, we can also direct the violet flame into conditions in our community or on the world scene—such as pollution, political turmoil or war—to transmute their karmic causes and bring resolution and peace. You can dedicate any of the affirmations above as well as the following prayer to bring about the highest resolution in any situation you name.

O violet flame, O violet flame, O violet flame!
In the name of God, in the name of God,
*   in the name of God!*
O violet flame, O violet flame, O violet flame!
Flood the world, and flood the world
*   and flood the world!*
In the I AM name, in the I AM name,
*   in the I AM name!*

Peace and peace and peace
*   be spread throughout the earth!*
May the Orient express peace,
May the Occident express peace,
May peace come from the East
*   and go to the West,*
Come from the North and go to the South,
And circle the world around!
May the swaddling garments of the earth
Be in place to magnify the Lord
In this day and hour and this night.
May the world abide in an aura of God peace!

Notes

KARMIC TRUTHS

1. See John 9:1–3 King James Version.
2. Matt. 17:11–13 New Revised Standard Version.
3. For an in-depth treatment of the role reincarnation played in the roots of Christianity and in the early Christian community, see *Reincarnation: The Missing Link in Christianity* by Elizabeth Clare Prophet with Erin L. Prophet (Corwin Springs, Mont.: Summit University Press, 1997).
4. See Elizabeth Clare Prophet, *The Lost Years of Jesus: Documentary Evidence of Jesus' 17-Year Journey to the East* (Corwin Springs, Mont.: Summit University Press, 1987).
5. Marvin W. Meyer, *The Secret Teachings of Jesus: Four Gnostic Gospels* (New York: Vintage Books, 1986), p. 50.
6. G. R. S. Mead, trans., *Pistis Sophia: A Gnostic Gospel* (Blauvelt, N.Y.: Spiritual Science Library, 1984), pp. 220, 315, 320, 220.
7. G. W. Butterworth, trans., *Origen: On First Principles* (Gloucester, Mass.: Peter Smith, 1973), pp. 137, 136.
8. Origen, quoted in Jean Daniélou, *Gospel Message and Hellenistic Culture,* trans. John Austin Baker (Philadelphia: Westminster Press, 1973), p. 418.
9. Ibid., pp. 418–19.

10. Butterworth, *Origen: On First Principles,* p. 67.

11. W. Lutoslawski, *Pre-Existence and Reincarnation* (London: George Allen and Unwin, 1928), p. 29.

12. Albert Schweitzer, quoted in Joseph Head and S. L. Cranston, comps. and eds., *Reincarnation in World Thought* (New York: Julian Press, 1967), p. 130.

13. Arthur Schopenhauer, quoted in Joseph Head and S. L. Cranston, comps. and eds., *Reincarnation: The Phoenix Fire Mystery* (New York: Julian Press, 1977), p. 296.

14. Gina Cerminara, *The World Within* (New York: William Sloane Associates, 1957), pp. 3–4.

15. Head and Cranston, *Reincarnation: The Phoenix Fire Mystery,* pp. 270, 271.

16. For an excellent anthology of writings on reincarnation from around the world, see Head and Cranston, *Reincarnation: The Phoenix Fire Mystery.*

17. Dr. Alexander Cannon, quoted in Joe Fisher, *The Case for Reincarnation* (New York: Carol Publishing Group, Citadel Press, 1992), p. 47.

18. Dr. Morris Netherton, quoted in Fisher, *The Case for Reincarnation,* pp. 41-42.

19. Robert L. Snow, *Looking for Carroll Beckwith: The True Story of a Detective's Search for His Past Life* (Emmaus, Penn.: Rodale Books, Daybreak Books, 1999), p. 7.

20. Ibid., pp. 1, 186.

21. Helen Wambach, *Reliving Past Lives: The Evidence*

        under Hypnosis (New York: Bantam Books, 1978),
        p. 6.
22. Gina Cerminara, *Many Mansions* (New York:
    William Sloane Associates, 1950), pp. 53, 52–53,
    55, 66–67, 65–66, 67.
23. Noel Langley, *Edgar Cayce on Reincarnation* (New
    York: Warner Books, 1967), pp. 49, 50–51.
24. Fred Ayer, Jr., "The Ancestral Shades of Gen. George
    S. Patton," *Fate,* March 1967, pp. 37, 38.
25. Kyle Crichton, *Subway to the Met: Risë Stevens'
    Story* (Garden City, N.Y.: Doubleday & Company,
    1959), pp. 237–38.

KARMIC THREADS

 1. For more on group karma and how it is sometimes
    expiated through nature, see *Saint Germain's
    Prophecy for the New Millennium,* by Elizabeth
    Clare Prophet with Patricia R. Spadaro and Murray
    L. Steinman (Corwin Springs, Mont.: Summit Uni-
    versity Press, 1999), pp. 121–47, 297.
 2. Dannion Brinkley with Paul Perry, *Saved by the
    Light: The True Story of a Man Who Died Twice and
    the Profound Revelations He Received* (New York:
    Villard Books, 1994), pp. 26, 52.
 3. Joel L. Whitton and Joe Fisher, *Life between Life:
    Scientific Explorations into the Void Separating One
    Incarnation from the Next* (New York: Warner
    Books, 1986), p. 48.
 4. Ibid., p. 39.

. Ibid., p. 44.

6. Ibid., pp. 44–45.

7. Christopher M. Bache, *Lifecycles: Reincarnation and the Web of Life* (New York: Paragon House, 1991), pp. 181, 182.

8. Langley, *Edgar Cayce on Reincarnation,* pp. 59–60.

9. Ibid., pp. 55–59.

10. Helen Wambach, *Life before Life* (New York: Bantam Books, 1979), p. 164.

KARMIC TRAPS

1. Wambach, *Reliving Past Lives,* p. 7.

2. Bache, *Lifecycles,* p. 130.

3. Whitton and Fisher, *Life between Life,* p. 53.

4. Ibid., pp. 47–48.

5. See Elizabeth Clare Prophet and Patricia R. Spadaro, *Alchemy of the Heart* (Corwin Springs, Mont.: Summit University Press, 2000), pp. 129–51.

6. Betty J. Eadie, *Embraced by the Light* (New York: Bantam Books, 1994), p. 99.

KARMIC TRANSFORMATIONS

1. Paramahansa Yogananda, *Autobiography of a Yogi* (Los Angeles: Self-Realization Fellowship, 1946), paperback ed., p. 349.

2. See Elizabeth Clare Prophet, *The Great White Brotherhood in the Culture, History and Religion of America* (Corwin Springs, Mont.: Summit Uni-

versity Press, 1984), pp. 173-206.

3. Yogananda, *Autobiography of a Yogi*, pp. 18⁷ 188-89.

4. Fritjof Capra, *The Tao of Physics*, 2d ed. (New York: Bantam Books, 1984), p. 141.

5. Hegel, quoted in Head and Cranston, *Reincarnation: The Phoenix Fire Mystery*, p. 19.

6. If you would like to learn more about how to put into practice the techniques of affirmation and visualization to access the violet flame, see Elizabeth Clare Prophet's audiocassette *Spiritual Techniques to Heal Body, Mind and Soul* published by Summit University Press.

We extend a heartfelt thank you to the wonderful team that helped nurture this book to completion, including Karen Gordon, Louise Hill, Lynn Wilbert, Virginia Wood, Judith Younger and Roger Gefvert.

For more information

Summit University Press books are available at fin bookstores worldwide and at your favorite online book seller. If you would like to receive a free catalog featurin our books and products, please contact:

Summit University Press, PO Box 5000, Gardiner, MT 59030-5000 USA. Tel: 1-800-245-5445 or 406-848-9500. Fax: 1-800-221-8307 or 406-848-9555

Email: info@summituniversitypress.com
www.summituniversitypress.com